JOHN B. OAKES

The Edge
of Freedom

Harper & Brothers · Publishers · New York

THE EDGE OF FREEDOM

Copyright © 1961 by John B. Oakes
Copyright © 1959, 1960 by The New York Times Company

Printed in the United States of America

FIRST EDITION

C-L

Library of Congress catalog card number: 61-6438

To Margery,
and Andra, Alison, Cynthia

Contents

Foreword

The purpose of this study is to stimulate thinking as well as to examine some of the political factors affecting two widely separated yet subtly connected parts of the world: the new countries of sub-saharan Africa and the Eastern European fringe states of Poland and Yugoslavia. It is, within a briefly descriptive framework, a critique of the American approach toward them and theirs toward us.

The Edge of Freedom has grown out of many interviews and extensive travel in Europe and Africa under a grant of the Carnegie Corporation of New York, with the generous co-operation of the *New York Times*. Some of the material has appeared in articles published in the *New York Times Magazine* in 1959 and 1960. The views expressed are entirely my own, and neither the Carnegie Foundation nor the *New York Times* is in any way responsible for them.

I wish to record here my deepest appreciation to my wife, Margery Hartman Oakes, without whose constant encouragement and assistance this book would not have been possible. I am also indebted to my friend Daniel Lang for his invaluable advice.

J.B.O.

New York, February, 1961

Introduction

The urge to reproduce his kind is the deepest instinct of every animal; the deepest instinct of many societies is to extend and reproduce the system they have evolved. The spread of an idea gives strength to those who hold it; it fortifies them in the conviction that they are right, lends assurance of continuity and hope of permanence.

It is the most natural thing in the world for us who believe in democracy to want to see it widely disseminated, and to help peacefully in its establishment wherever possible. It is also a matter of self-interest.

The clash of the two great power systems, one headed by the United States and the other headed by the U.S.S.R., each fortified by its own ideology, has tended to make us view the world around us in terms of black and white. If other countries were not "for" us, they were "against" us; and indeed during the height of the Soviet Union's most openly aggressive period after 1945—from the seizure of the Eastern European states to the Korean War—such sharp distinctions had some color of reality. But during the long period of the colder war since 1953, the special position of the uncommitted and the neutralist states has begun to evolve more clearly, as this type of state itself has been proliferating in the under-developed, formerly colonial areas of Asia and Africa. In the last five years it has become increasingly evident that these newer nations, and even one or two in the Communist world, are developing their own forms in their own patterns, thus requiring us to look at each one individually rather than as part of a monolithic whole.

The fact is that neither in the democratic bloc, the Communist bloc nor the neutralist bloc is there uniformity any longer, if there ever was. We tend to think of "democracies" as our kind of state, but the generic term covers countries with governmental systems as different as those of Canada and France, of Uruguay and South Korea. Even under the broadest possible definition of democracy, Franco's Spain could not be included; yet it is linked to the Free World, most particularly to the United States.

We should not be surprised—but many Americans do not seem ever to have thought of the possibility—that there are some notable variations in the Communist world as well. Soviet-style Communism is a far cry from Yugoslav Communism, and Polish Communism is different from both. It is too much to expect any of the states bordering Russia, which were Communized by the Soviet Union immediately after the Second World War, to renounce their ideological allegiance under the direct shadow of Russian guns; and in fact now the process of Communization has gone so far that it cannot be reversed. Even Yugoslavia, which was not on Russia's border, and did manage openly to declare its independence, has willingly retained its basic Communist structure.

But the point is that in Poland—and of course more so in Yugoslavia—the overwhelming weight of Russian domination has not been sufficient to suppress all independent growth and development. The same thing is true, though to lesser degree, in the other satellites. The variations have importance to us as Americans; for they suggest that it is a mistake to consider the Communist world as a gigantic unit, which can be adequately covered by one policy.

In most of the underdeveloped, non-Communist world, socialist-style welfare states have been established almost universally wherever the former colonial powers have withdrawn; and these new states also vary widely in every possible respect. There can be no single American policy that is right for Burma and also for Tanganyika, or for Vietnam and also for Guinea. The states of Asia and Africa are highly individualistic, and while the course of their early development under independence may be patterned after European forms, their growth to maturity will be molded by their own local conditions.

It would be wise to stop thinking about Africa and Asia as integral units and began thinking—a much harder job—about the countries of Africa and Asia as individual entities, each entitled to its own specialized attention. That is, it would be wise to follow this course if we expect to have any success in the pursuit of what must be our most basic policy vis-à-vis the new countries of the world: helping them gain their freedom now that they have their independence. The freedom they seek and must attain is a freedom from any kind of foreign political or economic domination, including our own.

The "neutralism" resulting from this upsurge of effort is a neutralism that can pose far greater problems in the long run for the Soviet Union than for ourselves. Genuine neutralism represents a serious barrier to the advance of Communist imperialism; and therefore the Sino-Soviet world is making every attempt to subvert genuine neutralism wherever it appears. From Cairo to the Congo, the U.S.S.R. is trying to misuse neutralism for its own purposes, while our interest is quite the opposite. We do not need to distort it; we can accept it so long as it is real. We have no desire for satellites, no ideology to export to the newly "neutralist" countries save liberty and freedom.

Our interest is not that they align themselves with us, not even that they practice the same kind of democracy that we do, though that of course would be gratifying. Our interest is rather that they be able to choose their own course without control by the Russians, by the Chinese or by ourselves. And if they pick a different kind of governmental system, or a different kind of economic system, we can get along with it so long as the choice is free. Ours is not the only kind of democracy, and it is not even necessarily true that full democracy is best for all peoples at every stage of their development, particularly the earlier stages. It takes a certain degree of sophistication to understand the value of giving "foreign aid" to countries that may not vote our way in the United Nations, or may not believe in the capitalist system or may not practice the style of parliamentary government to which the West has become accustomed.

With our older allies of the free world, we have an indissoluble community of interest founded on a historic, cultural and philosophic base, strengthened by the deepest political and economic ties. But with the newer states, relations inevitably are different. They require a different approach and different policies, related to their special position in a divided world. "I do not believe," said Dean Rusk, now Secretary of State, in his testimony before the Senate Foreign Relations Committee on January 12, 1961, "that we ourselves should be unduly concerned about what might be called the genuine neutralism because if a new nation is internally vigorous, viable, strong, progressive, its orientation in foreign policy is not so important as its health and strength. . . . I do not believe that we should insist that anyone who is not with us is against us."

Part I

CHAPTER 1

The New Role of Neutralism

The new role of neutralism is an increasingly vital factor in international relationships, especially between the more developed and the less developed parts of the world. It represents a growing point of contact among countries of widely divergent ideologies that, wishing to be part of neither East nor West, find themselves on common ground as they stand at the frontier edge of freedom.

Neutralism is so new a word in the current language of diplomacy that even in the latest (1961) unabridged edition of Webster's New International Dictionary it is given only a one-line reference as a rarely employed synonym of neutrality. But the dictionary is behind the times; and neutralism has now entered current usage with a special significance of its own.

Neutrality refers to the abstention of a state from a shooting war between two others, neutralism to the attitude of a state toward others in the absence of a shooting war. Neutrality suggests a legal condition or status during actual hostilities; neutralism a policy or approach in international relations in time of peace (or cold war). Neutralism implies not that the country practicing it sees no moral distinction between the opposing causes, but only that it does not feel bound as a matter of national interest to declare itself with one side or the other.

The United States followed a policy of neutralism (as well as neutrality) throughout our early history; but our tolerance of other people's efforts to pursue a similar course has progressively lessened during this century, until our growing postwar conflict with the Soviet Union finally reduced it to the vanishing point under the administration of the State Department by John Foster Dulles. Using the word "neutrality" (but in the sense that we today use "neutralism") Mr. Dulles as recently as June, 1956, could say that it "has increasingly become an obsolete conception and, except under very exceptional circumstances, it is an immoral and short-sighted conception."

Four years later, President Eisenhower said—in speaking to the heads of U.N. delegations of sixteen newly independent countries (fifteen of them African): "We do not urge—indeed we do not desire—that you should belong to one camp or the other [in the East-West conflict]."

The contrast is diametrical; the change in official thinking represented by these two statements could hardly have been more complete. It was caused by the belated realization that the world has suddenly become full of "neutralist" states and that American policy toward them was founded on conditions now obsolete.

This policy is still uncertain, still faltering, still ambivalent, as was well illustrated by the heavy-handed errors committed by the United States in respect to the three leading neutralists during the U.N. General Assembly session as recently as the fall of 1960. These three are Nehru of India, Tito of Yugoslavia and Nkrumah of Ghana, each an outstanding neutralist of his continent. Each was offended, each in a different way, by the United States. We led the battle—entirely unnecessarily—against Nehru's major U.N. effort to achieve an Eisenhower-Khrushchev meeting, and he went home rebuffed; we failed to invite Tito to Washington on his first visit to our country, and he went home disgruntled; we publicly accused Nkrumah of "very definitely leaning toward the Soviet bloc," and he went home to pursue those policies more ardently than ever. Clearly the validity of the neutralist position is being recognized only haltingly and with difficulty in the United States.

The neutralism expressed by many nations—especially the new ones of subsaharan Africa, with which this chapter is primarily concerned—is not a moral judgment, but a political one, a judgment that it is in their interest to stay away from the great power struggle. This does not mean that they do not know that there is a moral distinction between freedom and slavery, but it does mean that they do not believe it to their own benefit to align themselves automatically with the forces of freedom as we identify them in the West. It can merely mean that they see benefit to themselves in playing off one side against the other. It may also mean—something much more ominous—that they do not even believe that we always represent the forces of freedom. No matter how infuriating their judgments may be, the fact remains that a great many countries in the world are now assuming a neutralist position.

Their "neutralism" is often described as a "neutralism against us" because their votes in the U.N. are so frequently on the Russian side. But the vital difference is that they do not form an integral part of the Soviet bloc, which almost without exception casts its nine votes as one. Tito, Nehru and some of the other leading neutralists desire to avoid alignment with any bloc, and even deny the existence of a "neutral bloc." They conceive their role as one of independent but co-operative action with other neutralists, not of faithful commitment to a specific policy line that the word "bloc" implies. Yugoslavia, the "neutralist" in the most difficult position of all, rarely votes against the U.S.S.R.; but it does preserve in its attitudes some freedom of action and independence of decision.

This is not a meaningless distinction. The Yugoslavs are, after all, a Communist state and would naturally have views in most international matters similar to those of the Russians—on China and on Germany, for instance—but they are not necessarily slavish followers of the Russians. In at least two important votes at the U.N. in the fall of 1960, the Yugoslavs abstained while the Soviet bloc cast identical ballots, as usual. These were on the resolution to discuss alleged American "aggression" (based on the U-2 and other incidents), which failed 10 to 54, and the resolution to bring the disarmament issue directly into the Assembly, which also failed, 13 to 54. (In the first instance the only nation actually to vote with the Soviet bloc was Cuba, and in the second, Cuba was joined only by Guinea, Mali and Afghanistan.)

The existence of Yugoslavia as an independent Communist state outside Russian control—the living proof that such a thing is possible in Europe—is a matter of basic political significance for us. While neither the United States nor any other country can persuade the Yugoslavs to abandon their version of Communist society, they on their own initiative are moving further from Moscow's version every day.

More and more noticeably in the recent past Yugoslavia has been assuming a leading role in advancing the concept of neutralism. It is the only Communist state in Europe free enough to do so; and to Moscow's annoyance it has been vigorously pushing this idea in fertile ground in Asia and especially in Africa with loans and credits and diplomatic visits. The growth of a genuine neutralism free of Soviet inspiration and control in, for example, the newly independent countries of tropical Africa, could be a major embarrassment to the U.S.S.R. in its present efforts to dominate the policy of the less-developed states. It could also be a major boon to American efforts to encourage them in their independence.

The whole concept of neutralism has, in fact, taken on a new significance, both inside the United Nations and outside it, with the sudden emergence of formerly colonial territories as independent states. The process had been going on gradually since the close of the Second World War, first in Southeast Asia, then in Northern Africa and finally in the central segment of the African Continent. Neutralism, which a few years ago was looked on by many persons in the Free World as hardly more than a cover for pro-Soviet inclinations on the part of its practitioners, has developed into a positive factor of importance in international relations, and one that both "East" and "West" must reckon with. Though it is true that neutralism thus far has usually worked to our disadvantage, that will not necessarily remain the case.

More definitively than ever before, the neutrals expressed themselves as neutrals at the General Assembly's 1960 session. The most dramatic display of the new role of neutralism came with the abortive resolution of the five principal neutrals asking for a meeting between President Eisenhower and Premier Khrushchev as "an urgent first step" toward a *détente* in Soviet-American relations, which had deteriorated so rapidly since the collapse of the Summit Meeting in the spring.

The sponsors of this resolution, in which Tito played a major role, were India, Yugoslavia, Indonesia, Ghana and the U.A.R.— two Asian, two African and one East European state. Both Eisenhower and Khrushchev had set up conditions for such a two-power "Summit" meeting which the other would not accept, so that passage of the resolution would not have forced the United States (or, for that matter, the U.S.S.R.) into a meeting it did not want at that particular time. But while the U.S.S.R. abstained from active opposition to the resolution (and according to some reports secretly encouraged it), the United States took a leading behind-the-scenes part in weakening it, with the result that the resolution was angrily withdrawn by its sponsors and the United States shouldered the blame. Even had the resolution been passed, the meeting would not have been held; but through insensitivity to the currents of opinion in the neutralist world, the United States had once again succeeded in ranging itself against the leading neutralists, while the U.S.S.R., by keeping quiet, had remained out of this line of fire. The incident merely reflected the failure of American diplomacy to recognize a new and more flexible policy toward neutralism that has been slowly and reluctantly taking shape during the past few years.

This policy takes account of the fact that many of the underdeveloped countries see no direct threat from the Soviet Union or Communist China. They have had experience not of Communist colonialism but of Western colonialism. If they are blind to the danger arising from the growth of the former as the latter declines, most of them are at least sincere in their belief that they can now keep out of the clutches of both. In doing so, they also hope to remain aloof from the East-West conflict, and they are beginning to rely on their new power in the United Nations to keep it at arm's length. For it is in the United Nations that the new states are coming into their own; and the force of neutralism within the United Nations is rapidly changing the power balance within that body, bringing to it new strengths as well as new dangers.

The largest single geographic group in the General Assembly of the United Nations today is the group that calls itself Afro-Asian, consisting of nearly half the U.N.'s present membership. More than half of this Afro-Asian bloc is now African; and of the African group well over half achieved their independence during the year 1960 alone. Many of these states have retained very close ties with the European countries of which they were so recently colonies or protectorates: Senegal with France, for example; or Nigeria with Britain.

But the interesting thing about their voting in the General Assembly is that, by and large, they have refrained from taking either a pro-Russian or a pro-Western line. Guinea, which normally votes with the Soviet bloc, is an obvious exception; but even Guinea helped draft the resolution adopted 70 to 0 on Sept. 20, 1960, endorsing Secretary General Hammarskjöld's policy in the Congo, over bitter objections of the Russians (who, seeing they had no support in their attack on the Secretary General, abstained when the vote was counted).

Nigeria, for all its friendliness with Britain, has repeatedly assumed an entirely independent position quite at variance with Britain's; Cameroon, almost totally dependent on France, asked through its Foreign Minister in his first speech at the U.N. that the great powers "avoid the temptation to confront one another in Africa and to transfer there consequences of the war, hot or cold." On the Russian proposal to discuss America's so-called "aggressive acts," a number of African states opposed the Soviets; but all that British-oriented Nigeria and French-oriented Senegal and even U.S.-oriented Liberia did was to abstain. When the Western European powers and the United States argued against postponement of the elections to the Security and to the Economic and Social Councils, they were overruled by the strength of the Afro-Asians (supported by the Communist bloc) on a motion proposed by Nigeria and backed by all but two of the new African states. "We didn't bring Nigeria up to be a bloody neutralist," a British diplomat said; but it looks as though that is exactly what Nigeria will be.

The perfectly clear refusal of the new countries to side automatically with the democratic world against the Communist world may be shocking to our sensibilities, but it ought not to be viewed as a disaster. Quite the contrary. The very fact that the new countries vote as they please is proof that—even in this earliest stage of their freedom—they are acting as independent states, which is precisely the role that we had hoped they would assume once they emerged from their colonial status.

But the corollary of independence is responsibility. As sovereign members of the United Nations, the new African (and Asian) states have been plunged into the whirlpool of international politics in many instances before they have trained enough personnel even to swim through the rapids of domestic politics. They now have via their U.N. membership an influence on matters in which they cannot possibly have any real competence; yet they must play their role. They rightly demand respect as sovereign nations, but they have the reciprocal obligation of acting with a sense of responsibility toward the rest of the world and toward each other. They do not always do so; and some of them showed up very badly in the Congo dispute, in which to seize a momentary political advantage they followed the Soviet Union's line that could yet lead to wrecking the United Nations itself. The influence of Nasser is almost as dangerous; for under cover of "neutralism" he is attempting to pursue in Africa a policy of neo-imperialism, and to embrace a number of the smaller states in his increasingly pro-Soviet orbit.

It is fundamental to American interest—and to the interest of all the Free World—that the new states be nobody's satellites, neither ours nor the Soviet Union's. It is to our interest that they exercise their own judgment and their own free will in international matters;

and if they do we can be confident that—given a sensible American policy toward them—they will not voluntarily succumb to any kind of new colonialism, once having shaken off the old European variety. The emergence of states primarily concerned with their own political and economic development in peace and freedom can only strengthen the ultimate American aim of establishment of a world order of independent countries dominated by none, and equal in rights if they cannot be equal in power.

We are giving economic aid to the underdeveloped countries of Asia and Africa and Latin America not to buy votes in the U.N., but to help these countries stand on their own feet as independent entities, free enough to be neutral if they choose and free enough to resist Communist control as well as American domination. This is the crucial point; but it will become increasingly difficult to be guided by it as the new neutrals take increasingly independent positions.

There are certain specific doctrines that separate the neutralists from the United States and impel them to vote often alongside the Soviet Union in the U.N. The most ironic of all these issues is that of colonialism. We know, and they know, that the only dynamic colonialism today is Russian colonialism; but they know, and we ought to realize, that the only colonialism the African and South Asian countries have experienced in modern times is Western European colonialism. Furthermore, this latter type of colonialism, receding though it is, is still the only visible kind on the African Continent. To the Africans it is still evident in Algeria, in the huge Portuguese colonies of Angola and Mozambique, in the minor Spanish colonies and in British East Africa (where it is no longer a Colonial Office but rather a "white settler" kind of colonialism) and in the Union of South Africa. From the African point of view Western colonialism is still very much in evidence; and in this category the African includes the Negro civil rights problem in America.

Not only is it in evidence to the Africans, but it forms a primary wedge between the new African states on the one hand and the colonial and ex-colonial powers on the other. Even when relations are friendly, as in the case of most of the British and French colonies that have already received their independence, the memory of the past dies hard. While considering themselves neutral in the East-West struggle, most of the former colonies will find themselves lined up with the Soviet bloc—or, more accurately, find the Soviet bloc lined up with them—against the West on all matters touching colonialism. The tragedy is that we of the Free World are so frequently to be found on the other side.

"It is almost grotesque," Secretary of State Rusk said recently, "that when you walk into the General Assembly of the United Nations you see there the benches filled with delegates of independent members . . . who at one time or another were part of a Western political system; and yet Mr. Khrushchev makes some headway in trying to stand up as the champion of freedom at the expense of those of us who invented it."

Almost all the old colonial and formerly colonial countries are linked together in NATO, the keystone of American politico-military policy in Europe. While NATO is of vital importance to the United States in Europe ("our central and most important defensive alliance," as President Kennedy calls it), NATO has unnecessarily handicapped us in Africa because we have allowed our link with it to influence our African policy.

When the United States, along with only eight other countries, abstained from voting on the anti-colonialism resolution in the General Assembly late in 1960, we only emphasized a blind adherence to our allies' wishes at the expense of our own ideals and interests. On this resolution, which carried by vote of 89 to 0, the abstainers were the United States, Britain, France, Belgium and Australia—and Spain, Portugal, the Dominican Republic and the Union of South Africa.

Our abstention on this resolution was an egregious blunder, deplored both privately and publicly by some members of our own delegation. Our position was technically based on unacceptable language in the resolution, but it was taken (reportedly at President

Eisenhower's express command) almost certainly in order to re-main in line with our NATO allies who also are—or were—colonial powers. Whatever the reason, the damage this abstention did us throughout the underdeveloped and uncommitted world is incal-culable. And it will be long-lasting. For years American diplomats will be taunted by the fact that on a resolution opposing colonialism we were almost alone in the world except for our NATO allies and Spain and South Africa!

The advantage to the United States of NATO in Europe surely outweighs any disadvantage to the United States of NATO in Africa; but we would simply be overlooking a political fact of life if we overlooked the effect of NATO (and SEATO) on Afro-Asian attitudes toward us. That NATO is itself a guarantee to the small states of Africa, permitting them to assume the luxury of neutralism, is of course something that they do not recognize—or, if they recognize, do not admit.

As long as the United States refuses to dissociate itself from our NATO ally France on the subject of Algeria, or from our NATO ally Portugal on the subject of the Portuguese colonies, just so long will we be pilloried—along with them—as "colonialist." Our alliance with France is of prime importance and is unshakable; but it is questionable whether loyalty to that alliance should have pre-vented us from exercising our strongest influence to encourage the French in every way possible to reach the inevitable solution in Algeria.

There can be no question, however, that our alliance with Portugal, the one remaining European colonial power in the old-fashioned sense, is costing us more than it is worth. The United States has allowed itself to be hamstrung in its true anti-colonialism by our deference to the feelings of Portugal—an absurd case of the tail wagging the dog. In the U.N., the United States did not even dare to support a resolution directing Portugal to report "without further delay" on conditions in her overseas territories. While sixty-eight nations voted for it and six against, we, for fear of offending Portugal, abstained.

As long as the United States is thus untrue to her own ideals of freedom, we will stand condemned in the hearts and minds of millions of Africans as a colonialist power. Nothing we can say in extenuation will change that attitude; and the neutralists, aided and abetted by the U.S.S.R., will find themselves on these issues against us. The Soviet bloc has been pouring arms everywhere it could into Africa—into the U.A.R., into Morocco, into Guinea, into Ghana—but it is the use of American arms by the French in their warfare with the Algerian rebels that has excited the indignation of the African world.

Another source of neutralist resentment against the West, about which very little is heard in the United States, is France's use of the Sahara as a testing ground for its atomic bomb. This is a major issue in every country of West Africa, and all the French disclaimers in the world cannot still the fears of atomic dust carried by the winter wind, the harmattan, that blows south from the desert to the Gulf of Guinea. Although the scientific evidence shows that radioactive fallout from the first two French explosions ranged between 2/100 and 2/100,000 of the permissible dose, the Russians have played on African fears and have used them to stimulate a hatred of the "Western colonialists" that needs little stimulation. Five African states have in fact asked the U.N. to declare Africa a denuclearized neutral zone, from which any atomic weapons tests would be prohibited. And Nigeria, generally considered the most sophisticated of all the West African states, has actually ruptured relations with France over this issue.

Neutralism stems not only from political causes but from economic ones too. The Africans (and the Asians, for example in Afghanistan) have already seen that they can get economic help from both sides. In fact, the decision the Soviet government made a few years ago to embark on foreign aid is one of the most important policy decisions it could have made in the cold war. It has opened up limitless opportunities to the economic penetration of the underdeveloped world for obviously political purposes. The Russians do not even make a pretense of extending their aid through the U.N. What they have done on a multilateral basis has been minimal. They give bilateral economic aid for crudely political purposes; but they do it on such apparently generous terms (2.5 per cent interest, repayable in twelve years)—and they do it in such immediate response to need—that the underdeveloped countries find it almost impossible to resist even if they have the inclination, which most of them have not.

We are embarking on a hopeless and self-defeating course if in our efforts to hold Africa to our side we merely concentrate on keeping the Russians altogether out of that continent. To the extent that we overtly try to do so, we may well drive the new African states further toward the U.S.S.R. The tack should be not the negative one of keeping the Russians out—they are already in, in Ghana, in Guinea, in North Africa; and the Chinese are not far behind them —but the positive one of extending our aid to the new states to help keep them independent and make them free.

Still another factor basic to the neutralism of so many of the new states is their own political organization. Hardly any of the new and neutral countries is a Western-style parliamentary democracy. Most have assumed some form of welfare-state philosophy, with strong socialist and even authoritarian leanings. Except for relatively few French- and British-oriented intellectuals, the people of these states are no more tightly bound in ideology to the U.S.-NATO bloc than they are to the Communist bloc. By and large, their political, economic and social structure is taking shape on a basis of deeply rooted African tradition. The people of these countries cannot assume as a given premise that capitalist democracy is the best foundation on which to build their new society; they have no special predilection for "West" as against "East." In fact, there are some features of Communist political organization that may even fit more closely into African conditions than the forms of industrialized Western society.

The new role of neutralism needs to be understood by Americans; but to understand it does not imply that we must adopt it as a "cult" in which neutralists are per se given a higher place in the scheme of things than our own allies. A sensible view of neutralism suggests a balance: neither "exaltation of noncommitment"; nor its opposite, rejection of all who are not committed to our side; nor a third course, automatic acceptance of our allies' position even when the neutralists are clearly right.

Neutralism has to be looked at today as a new force in the world, to be approached with dignity but also without either moral resentment or immoral obsequiousness. As Dr. Henry S. Kissinger says, we are not engaged in a popularity contest; we must show sympathy and extend material aid for the underdeveloped countries in their legitimate national aspirations, and above all, "We must not expect that either our sympathy or our economic assistance will be paid for with short-term political support."

The great need for us is to be sufficiently mature to understand the need for neutralism even when we cannot bring ourselves to approve or to applaud it.

CHAPTER 2

The Sprouting Sovereignties

We have been unprepared for the rapid fade-out of the colonial empires since the Second World War, especially unprepared for the sprouting sovereignties of subsaharan Africa. We have been unprepared—through a combination of ignorance and indifference —for the emergence in patterns unfamiliar to us of indigenous regimes that are partly undemocratic, strongly socialist, mostly neutralist and largely undeveloped.

But if we have been unprepared, the states of Africa have been unprepared as well. The most unprepared of any of them—surely the most unprepared on the largest scale—is the formerly Belgian Congo. Yet all of them, poor in their new-found freedom (independence is the better word, for they are not yet really free), share certain major difficulties that spring out of the Africanism that is their common background and the colonialism that was their common fate.

Africa is not a unit in any sense: neither geographic, climatic, racial, cultural, linguistic nor historical. There are only Africas, vaguely defined by the points of the compass: North, South, East and West, alike only in their immensity and their emptiness. Even within these Africas, each huge enough to be a subcontinent in itself, there is no uniformity of terrain, of language, of custom, of civiliza-

16

tion. Algeria is as different from the Congo as Canada is from Brazil —and, incidentally, the distance from Algiers to Elisabethville is about as great as that from the St. Lawrence to the Amazon. For over five thousand miles this enormous continent stretches from the Straits of Gibraltar to Port Elizabeth.

One can fly for hour after hour over savanna or jungle or desert without seeing any sign of human population larger than the tiniest village. On the trip from Johannesburg to Brazzaville, for example, winging across the huge Portuguese province of Angola, the plane tops endless forests that cover the landscape as far as the eye can reach. Suddenly, a thin strip cuts through the trees, stretching from one horizon to the other like a fine gray wire laid on an endless sheet of green. It is the "line of rail" that runs from a Portuguese port on the Atlantic all the way across the continent and eventually to another Portuguese port on the Indian Ocean—fifteen hundred miles away. There is not a sign, along the single track, of a town or a factory or a house or a station, or even a train or an engine— just that one straight line cutting through the forest from nowhere to nowhere—a lonely cord to civilization in the endless expanse of Central Africa.

In a half-continent so vast as subsaharan Africa, generalizations are even more dangerous than usual, but it is still possible to identify some of the characteristics of tropical African states that make so difficult their rapid transition from colonialism to independence. Probably the most fundamental of all is that the structure of African society is tribal. Yet when the European powers during the course of the past three centuries carved up their colonial domains, they paid little or no attention to tribal boundaries but set the respective national frontiers at points selected merely to suit their own military, commercial or political convenience.

The result? There are today in tropical Africa few truly national states whose people have a long common and exclusive heritage of culture, religion, language or history. Every new African country contains many tribes; many of the tribes find themselves in two or more adjacent countries. In the Congo, for example, one of the principal ones extends through parts of former French and Belgian and present Portuguese territory.

For centuries before the Europeans came, the tribes fought savagely with one another as empires rose and fell. One of the benefits colonialism, with all its evils, brought to Africa, was a *pax coloniae*. Now that that is removed, tribal rivalries rise again to the surface; and in practically every country, as we see most clearly in the Congo, they form a centrifugal force. Coupled with it in West Africa is the religious separation of the Moslems of the dry interior from the non-Moslems of the humid coastal regions. This divisive factor was brought about centuries ago when the Moslem advance south from the Sahara was suddenly halted because, it is said, their horses were struck by the fatal tsetse fly as they entered the tropical forest.

Even in Ghana, where Kwame Nkrumah is hailed as "messiah" by the vast majority of the population, persistent opposition is based on tribal differences; and so Nkrumah has logically destroyed the power of the tribal chieftains whose local leadership might have threatened his. He has, in fact, tended to transform his country (as has his colleague in Guinea) into a kind of supertribal state.

The tribe is the unifying force in Africa, and it is the truly indigenous one. It was the structure of tribe, and beneath it the clan, the village, the family, that gave coherence to African life throughout the ages and up to the present day. African society had—and has—a collectivist base that often leads to the adoption of Marxist forms even when there is no conscious acceptance of Marxist doctrine.

After the advent of the colonialists, the various tribal governments remained more or less intact. The tribes each had their own chiefs, who ruled with the advice and consent of a council of elders. The chiefs were not absolute autocrats but were always subject to the dictate of custom and even to ouster if their rule was bad enough—a process known in West Africa as "de-stooling" because the chiefly authority was symbolized by a small and sometimes elaborately carved stool that no one ever sat upon.

The hierarchy of chiefs and subchiefs began at the village level where—because so much depended on the common consent of the elders of the village—a rough kind of democracy existed. And also a rough kind of socialism, in the sense that everyone was responsible for the welfare of all. It is logical that most of the new states are welfare states, stemming less from Marxism than from the African tradition of social responsibility. If democracy suggests consent of the governed, many of the forms of tribal government in Africa contained a primitively democratic understructure on which rested the extensive and apparently autocratic power of the chief.

The rapid development of these tribal societies into distinct nationalistic states could not have been expected to produce democracies in the Western sense, for all the democratic veneer acquired by the chieftaincy elite trained in England or in France. The truth is that the new countries are emerging from an incredibly low level of education and political experience in circumstances not remotely comparable to those of eighteenth-century America with its broad layer of sophisticated intellectuals, or nineteenth-century England with its extensive middle class. As the colonial empires of Africa die off, the new states are working their way out of the old cocoons—many before their time—in patterns quite unfamiliar and even alien to us. They are not producing true Western-style democracies; but they are not necessarily producing Western- (or Eastern-) style dictatorships either. The essential fact is that the new type of government in Africa is an African kind of government, neither European nor Asiatic.

Out of the problem of tribalism springs a related difficulty, the scarcity of nationally accepted leaders. There are some—Touré in Guinea, Nkrumah in Ghana, Nyerere in Tanganyika—but they are found mainly in the smaller states and not at all in such vast agglomerations of disparate entities as the Congo. The last thing the colonial rulers wanted to do in the earlier days was to raise Africans to genuine national leadership; and while the French pursued a policy of cultural assimilation, and in some favored localities gave political rights to the natives many years ago, it cannot be said that they deliberately trained an extensive crop of Africans competent to run with the ball of independence. An educated, Francized elite, yes, in such colonies as the Senegal; but a large body of potential leaders, no.

Nor did the British, though they permitted many a young tribal chieftain to tread the hallowed stones of Oxford or Cambridge, or, in more recent years, the not-so-hallowed ones of the London School of Economics. The British record is in this respect the best in Africa; and, while all things are relative, the comparative political advancement of Ghana and Nigeria bears testimony to the fact. The Belgians, of course, prepared no leaders of any kind—and neither have the Portuguese. The former have already paid, and the latter will surely pay, a terrible penalty for their neglect.

When the African leaders, such as they are, have managed to establish their authority, their rule inevitably appears to Western eyes as a dangerous approach to authoritarian dictatorship. The same pattern reappears: the single leader surrounded by his band of adherents, and enjoying a very broad measure of popular support; the single party dominated by the leader, and, in turn, dominating the legislature; the paraphernalia of democracy, including secret ballot, universal suffrage, perhaps an ineffective opposition; the mob hysteria and moral pressure directed toward achieving "popular" endorsement of the personalities in power; perhaps the use of force to ensure that the opposition (if any) is not too insistent; and even, here or there, the glimmerings of a neo-imperialism as a strongly organized country eyes its weaker neighbors.

The party or political grouping that has spearheaded the independence movement against the European suddenly finds that its victory over colonialism has also deprived it of the one truly unifying force among the African population. Previously suppressed rivalries, tribal, economic or political, now tend to make themselves felt, and are likely to erupt in a form violent enough to threaten the security as well as the unity of the state. This was precisely what happened in the Congo; it may easily happen wherever else the leaders are weak or their authority not universally recognized.

Superimposed on the problems of tribalism and of leadership is the frightening problem of economic survival. Except in the cities, where unemployment is extensive, most of tropical Africa does not suffer from overpopulation. Nor is it devoid of natural resources, though both its land and its people are eroded—the one through bad agricultural practices and the other through generations of disease.

What it does suffer from is almost total underdevelopment of all its resources, including the human. The most egregious failure of European colonialism was the failure to educate the African mass. The greatest need of Africa today, next perhaps to the need for responsible leadership, is the need for trained manpower. Not so much university-graduated manpower, important though that may be, but manpower competent to perform the multitude of administrative and technical services demanded by modern civilization, ranging from agronomist to zoologist, from merchant mariner to machinist, from statistician to schoolteacher.

The deficiency of technical and secondary education is startling. Primary education in Africa averages as much as 60 or 70 per cent in many places, but most primary teachers have hardly more than a primary education themselves. Secondary education is limited to but 2 to 3 per cent of the potential.

With human underdevelopment goes economic underdevelopment. There is not a single country in all of tropical Africa with per capita annual income as high as two hundred dollars, and in most of them it is less than half of that. The economies are based almost exclusively on production of raw materials for export and would therefore be dependent almost exclusively on fluctuations of world prices but for the considerable financial assistance extended by the former colonial powers. As it is, the largest of aid programs can be neutralized by a sudden drop in the international commodity markets.

Except for Ghana, which does quite well with its carefully controlled cocoa trade, it is hard to see how most of the new countries of Africa will be able to stand on their own financial feet for a long time to come. The former French Senegal, for example, has always been heavily dependent on a French subsidy for its one major crop, peanuts; even the mineral-rich Congo had in the two or three years prior to independence been running a deficit; Guinea had to sell its bananas some place, so it bartered them off to Soviet Russia and the satellites.

Inasmuch as there is hardly a state in all of tropical Africa that is self-supporting, the natural tendency of the newly independent nations is to seek economic strength in union. The French colonies had been grouped in colonial days in "French Equatorial" and "French West" Africa; today the eight or ten states that made up these groupings are trying to re-form them in limited degree, while carefully retaining their respective political identities (and the important jobs that go with the latter). The old French Sudan (Mali) is now linked with Ghana and Guinea. While these loose consolidations are based on economic needs, they also represent first steps toward a wider pan-Africanism.

With the growth of a money economy and the bare beginnings of industrialization, the cities of tropical Africa have mushroomed in size. Accompanying this trend toward urbanization, there has occurred a considerable "detribalization" among the natives, with its attendant social disorganization. When unemployment is mixed into this restless brew, potential street mobs, ripe for any kind of demagogy, result. Surely one cause of the disorder that erupted so violently in the Congo, where more than a third of the entire labor force are wage-earners, was that unemployment was heavy in the sullen capital of Léopoldville.

There is one more internal problem of fundamental importance that exists in some of the countries of tropical Africa, but fortunately not in all. That is the problem of race relations. Generally speaking, there is little real hostility on the west coast, for the good and sufficient reason that there are practically no permanent white settlers there.

The British were wise enough to forbid Europeans to carve out plantations in Nigeria; and the combination of the mosquito and torrid temperature kept them out anyway. Merchants, missionaries, civil servants, administrators were there aplenty; but they were and are only as flecks of foam on a great broad ocean of black humanity, estimated in such proportions as 1 to 2,000 in Nigeria, or 1 to 600 in Ghana.

But on the other side of the continent the story is different. The proportions of blacks to whites are "only" 100 to 1 in Kenya and only 12 to 1 in Southern Rhodesia. What is more important, many of the Europeans in those countries have settled on good agricultural land favored by temperate climate; they consider Africa their home; and they have been determined to maintain the political as well as the economic control they established when their fathers arrived a generation—or at most two generations—ago. As artisans or skilled workers, many of them—especially in the Rhodesias—have never been so well off.

These are the areas where segregation has existed as fiercely as anything known in Mississippi, where white supremacists (though they are not called that) have always held power, where economic discrimination is normal and political equality unknown. But even here the insistent voices of African nationalism are now loudly to be heard.

The color problem as such does not affect the internal management of most of the states of tropical Africa, but it does affect the perspective in which all of them view the outside world. The white man has been ineradicably linked in the African mind with the evils of colonialism; yet the relations of the emerging African states with their former masters have on the whole been excellent. (The Congo is, of course, the most spectacular exception, and Guinea is another.) But the memory of decades of white oppression has not yet been erased; and such incidents as "Little Rock" and "New Orleans," which many Africans know as symbols without precisely knowing what is involved, have served to revivify that memory.

This may be one reason why the Chinese have an appeal to some Africans, for they, too, are not white. To many African eyes they appear to be succeeding in an extraordinarily short time, at whatever human cost, in revolutionizing and industrializing their own country. The Communist Chinese have already established close relations with Guinea and with Ghana, and are already making important progress in the economic and diplomatic penetration of the continent.

They have given a $25-million interest-free loan to Guinea; they have agreed to provide technicians and specialists who—in an obvious dig at American practice—shall have a standard of living that "shall not exceed that of personnel of the same rank in the Republic of Guinea." The Chinese are frank about their intention to gain as large a foothold as possible in West Africa. A "Chinese-African Peoples' Friendship Association" has been established; "Afro-Asian Peoples' Solidarity Conferences" have been held; and the prospect for the future is unmistakably in the direction of more Communist Chinese influence, not less. What the Russians think about this is not known; but the result for Africa will surely be intensified Communist efforts from either source, or both.

Communism to most Africans does not have the deep significance it has to us. While Sékou Touré can speak as eloquently as any man on the subject of human rights and human freedom, neither he nor his people seem to be able to identify Communism with the new colonialism and the new imperialism. At least a partial explanation of this phenomenon springs from the egocentricity that particularly afflicts new nations still unsure of their status. In their insecurity, they tend to see all problems as centering in themselves; and they half-resent and half-fear others' failure to see these problems in precisely the same way. The Africans of the newer states have an intensely parochial view; it is the opposite of a world view, and they evaluate the U.S.S.R., the United States, the U.N. and every other force that touches them not on the basis of its impact on the world at large but as it affects them alone. This may be a perfectly natural reaction; but natural or not, it helps explain why the emancipated Africans (and Asiatics) so frequently fail to see the dangers of the Communist imperialism from which they have not personally suffered, and insist on the danger of a Western imperialism that they have felt in the past, fear in the present and yet that is obviously on the wane.

Strange as it may seem to us, the Russians come into Africa with what to many Africans, oblivious of Communist policy and practice throughout the world, looks like clean hands. The Russians and their satellites have stepped into every vacuum from Guinea to the Congo. Communist penetration has gone much further than direct financial aid. All along the West African coast, scholarships are scattered broadcast for study in Prague or Warsaw or Moscow, even Sofia. Technical advisers from Eastern Europe are appearing in Guinea and Ghana; industrial plants are being established; representatives of Communist news agencies (including the Chinese) are found with increasing frequency. Both Cameroon and the Congo have been plagued by terrorism verging on civil war, encouraged if not originated by Communist support.

There are some factors working against Communist penetration in Africa. The Russians and Chinese have, of course, no previous history in the continent, a fact that gives them the advantage of "innocence"; but it also gives them the disadvantage of inexperience. They have no record as African colonialists, but they also have no record as African teachers or administrators. The political, economic and cultural orientation of the African states toward Europe—above all, the use of English or French through most of central Africa—gives a base of common understanding that cannot outweigh the gross albatross of European "colonialism" but can mitigate its residual effect.

Furthermore, there are some indications that the Soviet Union may have overplayed its anti-Western hand in tropical Africa. While the powers of the Free World, particularly Britain and the United States, have been painfully learning the values of neutralism, Russia has been giving the impression of veering away from its former pretense of supporting "African solidarity" and a strictly neutralist position. It has seemed instead to be consciously pushing the "cold war" into Africa and to be forcing the African states against their will to choose sides. This newer tactic was evident first in the chaotic Congo situation, when the Russians unilaterally intervened while the United States operated scrupulously through the U.N. It was repeated in a different way when the U.S.S.R. vetoed Mauretania's application for admission to the U.N. It has been emphasized by the blatant supply of arms to selected states: to Guinea, to Morocco, to pro-Lumumba forces in the Congo. The Soviet Union may have decided that close friendship with and open supply of arms to a few countries in Africa—such as the United

Arab Republic, Morocco, Guinea, Mali and Ghana—might be worth more than championship of the underdeveloped nations in general.

These are the states that have consistently taken the most radical position on every question affecting Africa, and also the most anti-Western position. At Casablanca in January, 1961, they decided to form an African treaty organization patterned after NATO, "for the consolidation of liberty in Africa." These five states are not Communist; but with Nasser at their head, they have been increasingly pro-Soviet. The concentration of Soviet attention on them only reinforces the paramount necessity that Americans look on genuine neutralism not as something inherently evil for the underdeveloped countries, but rather as a stabilizing factor that will in the long run be to our benefit as well as to theirs. Soviet determination to make a power play for certain selected states may yield early dividends; but eventually it can only demonstrate to all Africa, including these same states, that the whirlwind of aggressive, bellicose imperialism now blows unmistakably from the Eastern quarter.

CHAPTER 3

"Devil with a Slavic Accent": Guinea

The city of Conakry stretches its long palm-fringed peninsula out into the bay that forms as beautiful a harbor as can be found in all West Africa. The setting sun disappears behind the green islands of Los sheltering Conakry's roadstead from the sea. Twinkling across the water are the lights of a Canadian ore boat, tied up at the island quay to receive its cargo of bauxite from the open mines. Pirogues, the long native dugout canoes, dart here and there like water insects in the twilight. From the airport comes the distant roar of the evening plane taking off for Dakar, 450 miles to the north. Night settles over Conakry—its waterfront, its half-dozen French-built skyscrapers, its comfortable tropic houses erected for Europeans but now inhabited by officials of the Guinea government, its crowded native quarter of mud-walled, tin-roofed huts that look not much better or much worse than those of any other native quarter in the tumescent cities of West Africa.

But Conakry is different, not because it is bigger—it is small as African capitals go; not because it is dirtier—its open squares and myriad trees and shiny beaches and harborside drives even make it

27

look cleaner than most; not because it is livelier—it can't hold a candle to Lagos, or Accra, or Dakar. It is different because it is the capital of a Soviet-oriented state that—unlike Gabon or Ghana—had no Western power to guide it through the infancy of its independence.

When "Guinée française" became the Republic of Guinea in October, 1958, the French proceeded ruthlessly to cut themselves off from their former colony. As was the case with every other major French colonial possession, the 2½ million Guineans (who boast the highest birth rate in the world) had been given by President de Gaulle the choice of voting to accept the newly projected French Communauté or reject it. Under the fiery leadership of their dynamic young left-wing leader, Sékou Touré, they voted overwhelmingly against it—the only state to do so. And that meant independence. Although he himself had offered them this alternative, President de Gaulle was furious over their decision to opt out. His fury began even before the referendum, when on a visit to Guinea Touré welcomed him with a remarkably undiplomatic speech to the effect that Guinea preferred freedom in poverty to economic security in slavery. The story is that de Gaulle promptly canceled a state dinner scheduled for that same evening and left Guinea without speaking to Touré again.

After Guinea rejected membership in the Communauté, most of the French civil service was withdrawn, and the filing cabinets and telephones to boot, as a mark of de Gaulle's displeasure. Sékou Touré and his brother Ismail, though descendants of a noble tribal house, had had early and strong connections with the Communist-dominated French Confederation of Labor. The combination of their leftist look and the Guineans' extreme animosity toward the French lessened any inclination to extend help to Guinea that the other Western countries might have entertained. The inclination was minimal at best, because the United States and Britain were at this moment having difficulties with their principal NATO partner, and they had no desire to do anything that would further irritate de Gaulle.

"We repeatedly tried to get help after independence," one of the highest officials of the government recalled a year later. "Our very first envoy went to France, the second to Washington. It was only when these requests for diplomatic, financial, commercial, technical and cultural accords with our new government were rebuffed that we turned to the East. The U.S.S.R. and the other Eastern European states promptly helped us. Of course, we welcomed that help, which came in the form of recognition of trade missions, of purchase of our banana crop that the French used to buy, of technical assistance, of everything we wanted. From the first day of independence, the door has been as wide open to the West as to the East; but only the East walked in." He paused a moment, then added: "We'd take aid from the devil himself; and we don't much care if he has a Slavic accent."

The first ambassador to be accredited to Guinea was the Bulgarian. The first loan to be granted to Guinea by a non-African state was Russian. It was a $35-million twelve-year credit on extremely generous terms. The second was Communist Chinese: $25 million, interest-free. The first trade agreements were not with France, which would have been natural, but with Czechoslovakia, Hungary, Poland, East Germany, the U.S.S.R. A new monetary system has taken Guinea out of the franc zone, reversed her pattern of trade from nearly total dependence on France to almost total independence, with the result that the bulk of Guinea's agricultural exports —coffee and bananas—are now going to Eastern Europe, and the bulk of her manufactured imports are coming from that source. Rice, a staple of Guinea's diet, will be arriving from China under a recent trade agreement, and with it a goodly quantity of "educational and cultural supplies." Guinea is exporting students to Eastern Europe, outnumbering those going to the West by a ratio of five or ten to one.

The wharves of Conakry are piled high with mysterious crates labeled "Made in Czechoslovakia." The railroad and the airport are being modernized by the Russians. It is reported that the U.S.S.R. is establishing a submarine base on the Guinean coast—an extremely ominous development if true. It is certain that arms and jeeps and buses and uniforms and equipment have come from Eastern Europe.

It was estimated early in 1961 that nearly one thousand Communist "technicians" have arrived in Guinea.

Conakry's one reasonably comfortable French-built and French-owned hotel is crowded with East Europeans drinking Czech beer and Czech wine. A Tass correspondent has settled down in Conakry to compete with the only resident Western newspaperman, who represents Agence France Presse. Guinea is, incidentally, one of the few independent countries of the world with neither a daily nor a weekly newspaper—not too surprising in view of its 90 per cent rural population and its 90 per cent illiteracy. The East Germans are building a printing plant now to supply the deficiency in newspapers, not to mention other forms of Communist propaganda.

The American Chargé d'Affaires did not even arrive until February, 1959—four months after independence. The Ambassador got there four or five months after that. It took the French three months to recognize Guinea, and many more months to work out the details of financial and commercial and cultural accords that would naturally have stemmed from the historic Franco-Guinea relationship.

The total American help to Guinea in 1959 consisted of five thousand tons of rice, three thousand tons of flour, and one schoolteacher (though English has been officially declared the country's second language). On the day the rice was delivered at Conakry's docks, a shipment of similar size was landed from Communist China. In 1960, a million dollars' worth of surplus agricultural commodities, 20 or 30 teachers and 150 scholarships were made available—small potatoes compared to the Soviet effort but nonetheless significant of a belated American interest in Guinea. One of the most serious stumbling blocks to American aid has been the standard American requirement that all U.S. technicians have both diplomatic privileges (duty-free imports) and diplomatic immunity—something that other aid-giving countries apparently do not demand.

The French, still smarting from the severance of Guinea from the Communauté, have assiduously promoted the view that it is already a Communist-controlled country. But not all Western observers share this opinion and certainly the Guineans themselves do not subscribe to it.

"We're not Communist; we're *communitaire*," claims President Touré as he relaxes in his air-conditioned office on the second floor of what used to be the French Governor's palace overlooking the bay. By this he suggests that his party-state is founded not on Marx but on something that has a superficial resemblance to Marx, yet is far older than Marx. That something is the ancient African tribal tradition based on the village community. Before and during colonial days the villages were ruled by elected councils which advised the chiefs. Now the real power of government is centered in the Guinean Democratic party (PDG). The local party officials are elected at the village level, thus forming a popular base for the party heirarchy.

"The party is the expression of the mass," says the PDG's general secretary. "This is the directing force that runs the country. The government itself—ministers, administrators and the like—are mere technicians. They can't impose their will on the party and through the party on the government." Succinctly declares the president of the National Assembly: "The state is the instrument of the party."

Though there was more than one party before independence, there is only one in Guinea today. In the first national election (held in January 1961) Touré won a majority of 99 per cent. This doesn't mean that Guinea is Communist; it does mean that it is authoritarian. As one experienced Western diplomat in Conakry observed: "Authoritarianism on a communal base is nothing more than traditional Africanism."

"Our revolution is not ideological anyway," President Touré insists. "We are not interested in ideology but in how to improve the conditions of the people of Guinea." One way of accomplishing this purpose has been to bring all exports and imports under the close control of a single governmental agency called the Comptoir Guinéen, which has thus gained the power of life or death over the big European-owned private trading corporations that flourished here as everywhere else in West Africa. Now they are being gradually pushed out as the channels of government-directed trade shift primarily toward Communist-controlled Europe and as the government-backed co-operatives take over more of the function of distribution and agricultural production.

Though most of the French civil servants left Guinea at de Gaulle's behest after independence, some two thousand Frenchmen of the original seven thousand still hang on—mainly merchants and businessmen and planters. They are not molested; but they aren't happy. "We're being squeezed out," says the manager of one of the big importing and distributing firms, as he sips his *apéritif* at the attractive beach club where French and Guinean society likes to gather. "All imports and exports are now controlled by the state organization. We have to buy certain items from Eastern European countries if we want to buy them at all—that's due to the trade and barter agreements, of course. We have cut our staff by 50 per cent, and it's still going down. The government is going to push us out by degrees."

"Yes," another one chimes in, "the smaller commercial and business enterprises are sure to go, though there has been little nationalization or boycott of French firms—yet. But the big operations, such as the bauxite mines, are safe." There are two such major enterprises in the country, both financed by Western capital and run by Western engineers, and tapping a reserve believed to be one-fourth of the world's total. The mines have been untouched by the change in government. "No nationalization is envisaged in industry or commerce," says President Touré. "We need and want to encourage foreign investment." No matter how socialist any of the West African states—Guinea, Ghana, Nigeria or the others—may theoretically be, they all recognize the need for outside capital and they all have great development schemes involving huge dams, hydroelectric plants—and much foreign money. However, the country's two major utility companies (partially French-owned), one supplying power and the other water to Conakry, have in fact recently been nationalized.

One form of investing that has been developed in Guinea is its program of "human investment," i.e., twenty days a year of "voluntary" labor by some 70 per cent of the population. Yet President Touré declares with every evidence of sincerity that "no system is good if it isn't planned within the framework of liberty—for man deprived of his liberty is no longer a man." By liberty, Touré means not only personal liberty of Guineans inside Guinea, but of all Africans from any form of colonial domination. His own government's record of violence against the meager opposition belies his words.

Urgent as are the problems of internal economic and political advancement, the unity of West Africa and its independence from colonialism are what is uppermost in official Guinean minds.

"The most important Guinean problem is Africa," remarks a ranking minister of government in his comfortable home in the residential quarter that used to be reserved largely for French administrators. "We can't be truly independent unless all Africa is independent. We want to stay out of the East-West quarrel. That doesn't concern us—but Africa does." As for the United States: "You had great credit here after the war—but when we see you line up in support of the colonial powers, France especially, on such African issues as Algeria and Cameroon, how can you expect us to remain friendly? If the United States feels that its relations with France or Europe are more important than its relations with Africa, that's understandable, but don't blame us for looking on you as being allied with our enemy."

"There's something else you ought to remember," he adds in his impeccable French. "The Negro question in the United States is of more concern to us than any theoretical question of Communism in Africa."

"But," he is asked, "how can you close your eyes to the fact that the most aggressive colonial power in the world today is not a Western European country but Soviet Russia?"

"Well, the Eastern bloc may be colonialist—but it hasn't colonized Africa, and it's Africa I'm concerned about. Why should I fear what you call Communist imperialism? We in Africa have had experience of French colonialism, of British colonialism, of Belgian and Portuguese; we know you Americans are allied with the British and French and Belgians and Portuguese. We have never experienced Russian colonialism or seen evidence of Russian imperialism. We can worry about Russia later; first we must rid this continent of the colonialism that still exists here—in Algeria, the Portuguese possessions, South Africa, Rhodesia."

"Besides," he continues, "even if you describe as colonialism Russia's control of its border territories, I'd take that kind of colonialism any day to the kind we experienced under France. Do you realize—" and the voice of this French-trained African, more at home in Paris than in the African bush, rises in passion—"do you realize that the French provided no higher education for this entire country, there was virtually no industry, no commerce except in French hands, no rights for the natives, no encouragement of our culture; we weren't even citizens? Call the Russians colonialists— but when I visited such Russian 'colonies' as Azerbaijan, I saw universities and technical schools, factories and folk art, handsome buildings and busy people. The French left us a legacy—of nothing."

The visitor realizes this is not quite true as he follows the fine waterfront drive that winds along the peninsula on which Conakry is built. He notes the modern skyscrapers, both business and apartment buildings, that grace this attractively located little city. He walks past the busy docks where a freighter is taking aboard a cargo of bananas; he looks across to the ore boats waiting to pick up their loads of rich red bauxite. The legacy of the past is visible and it is French. The promise of the future cannot be French; but Guinea is not quite yet lost to the world of freedom.

CHAPTER 4

Following the Leaders: The Two Malis

In the ancient tradition of chieftaincy, the peoples of Africa are prone to follow their leader; and the less sophisticated they are, the more they are likely to follow him. This leadership principle is not only normal in the present stage of African development, it is inevitable. Without deeply rooted parliamentary institutions, the respective states would be suffering from a vacuum of power were it not for the handful of leaders—the supratribal chiefs—who have been able by eloquence, arms or personality to rally most of the people about them. The tragedy is that there are not more leaders, and of higher quality; but that lack is not the fault of the Africans alone.

The leadership principle makes it difficult to establish a close pan-African union, for each local leader wishes to be the leader of all; and the followers of each will give their loyalty only to him. This is one reason why, language difficulties aside, the Ghana-Guinea-Mali union is so tenuous. It is one reason why the Federation of Mali, composed of Senegal and Sudan, could not survive. The people tend to take their cue from the leader and follow him with docility through every twist or turn of his political snake dance, no matter how rapidly he may double back on his tracks.

The brief history of the Mali Federation furnishes an example. Along with the people of every other major former French colony in Africa (save only Guinea) the population of the two West African states of Senegal and Sudan voted overwhelmingly in favor of the Communauté in September, 1958, as their leaders told them to. When in January, 1959, the respective leaders of the two countries formed a federation, their people backed them. When—to the surprise and annoyance of the French—the same leaders decided during the subsequent months that the time had already arrived for complete independence, their people gladly approved. Just sixty days after the independence of the joint Federation had been proclaimed, a bitter dispute between these leaders resulted in its dissolution; and their respective people followed them faithfully, as usual. Mali might have eventually broken up in any event; but the personal rivalries between the leaders of its two component parts was the primer that set off the explosion.

The Mali Federation was originally created within the Communauté out of France's oldest African colony, the Senegal, and its larger but poorer landlocked neighbor, the Sudan. The Senegalese have long had special privileges of French citizenship that set them apart from other West African colonial peoples, including those of the Sudan. More than forty years ago, Senegal sent a native deputy to the French Parliament; and the first African to enter a government of the French Republic came from Senegal in the 1920's. Dakar, capital of Senegal (and also of the short-lived Federation), is by far the most French of all African cities below the Sahara. Like all the others, it has its native quarter—as crowded, noisy and squalid as any; but more than any of the others, it has the atmosphere of a southern French provincial town, with large and businesslike buildings rising up above the harbor and the bright blue sea.

Diagonally across the street from the former palace of the French High Commissioner General, towering above the magnificent roadstead of Dakar, is the impressive skyscraper that used to house the French administration, and subsequently the governments of Mali and of the Senegal. Here it was easy to learn why the Communauté as originally conceived in terms of autonomy without independence was heading toward failure.

"When we voted for the Communauté, we thought we would be on a basis of equality with France," said one of the ranking ministers as he sat in his luxurious office with its superb view of the harbor behind him. "We found it didn't turn out that way. We expected a genuine partnership of whites and blacks. But the French organized it so the French would control. We discussed; but we had no effective vote. Within the Communauté our advice was not asked; we were informed of what was happening. The Communauté was run by the French and for the French, with French flag and French anthem. It was impossible to function under these conditions. We decided to exercise our option to achieve independence—within the Communauté if we could, outside it if we had to."

General de Gaulle, supreme pragmatist that he is, recognized the force of the demand for independence led by Mali. While the original conception of the Communauté had no room for independence at all, de Gaulle quickly reversed his field and worked out a strictly practical, Gaullist solution not only for Mali but for all the rest of subsaharan Africa. Something new was invented: a Communauté of independent states, similar to but not precisely the same as the British Commonwealth.

"We aren't going to cut our ties with France," said a Senegalese official. "We can't because we have neither the financial power nor the administrative personnel to get along without the French; nor do we have the desire. But we want to be on a true basis of equality, and we want to achieve it in orderly and friendly fashion. We feel linked to the West through France; but let me tell you that there is nothing to stop us from turning toward the East if the West ignores us."

And so independence was achieved in June, 1960, but, as it turned out, at the cost of Mali unity. As a merely autonomous state within the Communauté, Mali had managed to hang together; as an independent federation, its internal disruptive forces were too great. Senegal had the cultural contact with Paris, long experience in at

least some form of self-government, a relatively prosperous economy based on France's subsidy for Senegalese peanuts and on the
business and commercial interests centered on Dakar, West Africa's
greatest port. Sudan had 60 per cent more population (3.7 million
to 2.3 million) and six times the area; it also had a far less developed
people and an economy dependent on livestock. The Sudanese
favored a more centralized and stronger federal state than did the
Senegalese, who feared domination by their larger but less developed
partner.

In recognition of Sudan's predominance in size, the Sudanese
leader Mobido Keita was named Premier of the Federation. The
President was expected to be a Senegalese, Leopold Senghor, a distinguished poet. Just before the scheduled election in August, Keita
took steps interpreted as an attempt to block Senghor. The immediate response of the Senegalese was to declare the Federation
dissolved. This was on August 20, 1960—two months to the day
after the independence of this Federation had been proclaimed; and
a month later the Sudan (which had meanwhile taken over the
name of Mali) and Senegal were admitted as separate states to the
United Nations.

The breakup of Mali illustrates how difficult it is even for African
countries closely linked in cultural overlay, in religion, in geography,
in language to remain united against the opposing attractions of
personal rivalries, not to mention tribal jealousies and economic
disparities. It had been an uneasy union at best; for the more
sophisticated Senegalese were generally moderate in view and more
democratically oriented, even tolerating a political opposition. In
Sudan, however, one party has been in control from the beginning,
in much the manner of Sékou Touré's Guinea, a leader and a state
toward which many Sudanese inclined.

Under Mobido Keita, who is himself pushed by forces further to
the left, Mali has moved steadily away from French influence and
closer to the neutralism of Guinea and Ghana. It has for all
practical purposes left the Communauté; and already France has
been asked to evacuate its four army and air bases in Mali. French

financial aid has continued, and a few hundred French technicians remain; but Mali's unswervingly hostile attitude toward French policies makes the continuance of such aid uncertain.

In striking contrast to American immobility after Guinea's break with France is the positive action the United States took even before Mali had declared its independence. The American Consulate in Bamako, Mali's capital, was the first foreign mission in the country; and the first embassy after independence was the American. This is a hopeful indication of the growing awareness that even neutralist states that assume strongly anti-Western positions—as Mali did at the Casablanca conference early in 1961—must be approached with understanding rather than disdain.

Mali's outlet to the sea, apart from Dakar, can only be through Guinea or the Ivory Coast. But the latter state has been traditionally pro-French, and so political logic seemed to suggest a closer union of Mali with Guinea. However, Guinea was in no position in 1960 to lend needed funds to Mali, while Guinea's ambitious partner Ghana was. So late in the year, President Nkrumah of English-speaking Ghana was able to announce a legislative union with French-speaking Mali, cemented by a loan. As usual, the people of Mali followed their leader in this new direction.

As Ghana was already linked with Guinea in a looser kind of union, the net effect of the latest move is to create a strange kind of hybrid. Guinea and Mali border each other but Ghana is separated from both by the French-oriented Voltaic Republic and the Ivory Coast. This tripartite agglomeration may not last (although Ghana's economic power should help hold it together); but it represents, as long as it does last, a step—though a very tenuous one—toward Dr. Nkrumah's ambition for a West African federation, which he himself would like to head. So would Guinea's President Touré.

CHAPTER 5

Oldest of the New: Ghana

Standing in front of the National Assembly Building in Accra is a more than life-sized statue of Kwame Nkrumah, inscribed "Founder of the Nation." On the coins and postage stamps and billboards of Ghana are portraits of Nkrumah. The principal avenue in the capital city is named for Nkrumah, and so is a traffic circle with a fountain in the middle. The national decoration for valor is the Nkrumah Cross; for service to Africa, the Nkrumah Prize. The handsomest country residence on the steep ridge behind Accra, overlooking the hot coastal plain and the warm blue sea, belongs to Kwame Nkrumah, "Victorious Leader" and President of Ghana.

Technically a two-party parliamentary democracy, Ghana is practically a one-party state—even a one-man state. The first of Britain's African colonies to become independent (1957), it is a republic within the Commonwealth, with a brand-new authoritarian constitution approved by 88 per cent of the electorate in the spring of 1960 over a bitter, courageous but totally helpless opposition.

The man who runs Ghana—described by his more effervescent followers as "The Savior, the Torch, the Teacher, the Leader, the Miracle of the Twentieth Century . . . whose personality blackens out the most blinding of neon signs"—is Dr. Kwame Nkrumah, head of state, head of government, head of party. He holds all executive powers; he can dissolve Parliament, veto legislation and dismiss civil servants. He and a small group of advisers (mostly in the cabinet) decide what to do, and get whatever additional authority they need to do it from their Convention People's Party which has over 80 per cent of the seats in Parliament.

One of the things they have done in the four years of Ghana's independence is to enact a series of security regulations almost extinguishing Ghanaian civil liberties. At the top of the list is a Preventive Detention Act under which several dozen people are serving prison terms of up to five years without hearing, trial or appeal. Under another law, summary imprisonment or deportation for consistent dissemination of "false reports" is possible. Work groups for youth, so-called "builders' brigades" bearing a superficial resemblance to the American CCC of the thirties, are allegedly being used for parapolitical purposes. There is occasional intimidation at the polls. Constitutional safeguards, guaranteeing some measure of regional autonomy, have been whittled away. The ancient power of the local chiefs has been all but destroyed. The party, as the instrument of Nkrumah's will, is supreme, and he himself describes the government as only the "agent" of the party.

"I don't like laws that permit imprisonment without trial," says a high official of the Ghana government who received his Oxford accent at Cambridge a few years ago. "But you have to recognize that a new state such as this inevitably feels insecure. Even you Americans had your 'alien and sedition' laws in your early days. A plot was uncovered in 1958 against the life of our Premier; you will recall that in 1959 assassins murdered the Prime Minister of Ceylon. We have to take drastic steps to ensure our own security. Once that is firmly established, once the scattered opposition knows it cannot subvert the state by violence, then we'll be able to afford liberalism and do away with these distasteful restrictions. But that time isn't yet."

Says another English-trained Ghanaian in the civil service: "The one thing the enemies of African independence want to see is instability in the new African states. The moment we show any signs of internal disorder, they'll all say, 'See, the Africans aren't fit to govern themselves.' That kind of propaganda we're determined to prevent here. We're going to have order first; then we can have democracy. Look at the Congo; it has neither."

Nkrumah has managed to establish a strong, stable and unitary state, but the security problem remains real to the leaders of the Ghanaian government. They know that the inter-tribal and regional hostility that divided the peoples of the old Gold Coast before the British arrived is still persistent, in the face of Nkrumah's firm determination to create a truly national state built around one party —his—as a kind of supratribal organization. Actually, what he has been doing is to translate African tribalism into national terms, on a national scale; and then go it one better by imposing outright authoritarianism on top of it. Even if they had understood this, it would have made no difference to the tribal traditionalists who continue ineffectively to oppose him, along with a few genuine democrats. But their voice is small and their influence feeble.

Though Ghana has the unusual advantage of possessing one language group that is spoken by perhaps two-thirds of the population, it is plagued by the usual tribal and regional differences that affect almost all West African states. It has an extremely backward, aboriginal north, where as recently as five years ago there was not even one secondary school. The Ewe on the Togoland border, who consider themselves superior to the other tribes (K. A. Gbedemah, Ghana's Finance Minister and conceivably successor to Nkrumah, is an Ewe), the warlike Ashanti, the Ga "aristocracy" of Accra, are among those who give to the "people's government" of Nkrumah serious separatist problems which it has largely succeeded in surmounting. Nkrumah has neutralized the centrifugal power of the traditional tribal chieftains, and he has all but quashed effective regional opposition to centralized government. In the process, it was natural that he would meet with resistance in the form of plots, subversive movements and ordinary democratic opposition. The Preventive Detention Act was the result.

That the government itself has an uneasy conscience over having adopted and employed laws for summary arrest and imprisonment without trial is evident from its explanation:

> Put in its simplest form the question is this: is it better to adopt the type of laws which exist in many other democratic countries but which result in it being possible to restrain or imprison those believed to be involved in subversive activities although they have not been proved by the ordinary process of law to have committed any offence, or is it best to accept the risk of the overthrow of a democratic regime by refraining from taking any special methods for dealing with the threat? If special methods are taken in dealing with the threat, then, of course, these are quoted as examples to justify repressive measures taken in countries under arbitrary rule or colonial domination. If, on the other hand, special methods are not taken and as a result the State collapses, arbitrary Government and colonial rule can equally cite the result as an example for the continuance of arbitrary or colonial regimes.
>
> (Government White Paper—10-59)

Some of the leading oppositionists are in jail, but there is an opposition press (subject to censorship) in the shape of one outspoken daily, the *Ashanti Pioneer*, published in the Ashanti stronghold of Kumasi. The new university near Accra, designed to take an enrollment of one thousand beneath its incongruously Oriental-styled roofs, is a center of intellectual opposition, even though most of its students are indentured to the government for a period after graduation. Yet Nkrumah clearly has the support of the mass of Ghana's seven million people, who, because of the carefully controlled cocoa trade, enjoy the highest per capita income in subsaharan Africa.

The state Nkrumah and his followers are creating is socialist, with the government participating in every important enterprise. Diamonds, gold, manganese and timber are exported; but cocoa is the foundation of Ghana's economy (Ghana produces almost a third of the world's output). The government buys the entire crop from the thousands of small growers, and sells it at a much higher price in the world market—using the substantial differences as a major source of revenue.

This profit (or tax) is financing large-scale and generally well-planned investment programs, including roads, education and agricultural improvements. It is also financing some questionable projects, such as the Ghana air force with its proposed thirty-two jet fighters and ten-million-pound air base, or the million-dollar "minesweepers" bought for fishing patrols though they could probably have been had free of charge from Britain or the United States if Nkrumah had not been too proud to ask for them.

An American aid mission is spending about one million dollars a year in Ghana, mainly on agricultural extension work; and the United States has indicated its readiness to grant a large loan for the huge Volta River hydroelectric and aluminum-producing project in which American capital is heavily invested. There is also effective Soviet-bloc penetration both through industrial assistance and on the military, cultural and intellectual level, ranging from construction and equipment of factories and advice on how to run state farms to the supply of military airplanes and the awarding of technical and vocational scholarships in Eastern Europe. Though Soviet diplomats were not allowed into Ghana for two years after independence, they are now making up for lost time. The Soviet Union has granted a $40.6-million long-term credit to help develop Ghana's resources, and is supplying the technical assistance for Ghana's second-largest dam. Ghana and Communist China have already entered into formal diplomatic relations.

The most interesting example of foreign penetration, however, is that conducted by Israel in Ghana and in no less than fifteen other African states. Israel has, in fact, sent over 150 technicians to twenty-eight countries in Africa, Asia and the Middle East, but Africa has had the lion's share. The Israelis are not merely seeking an outlet for commercial products, though they are doing that too. More specifically, they are seeking to build up in Africa friendly relationships with other countries of the continent that may serve as a counterweight to the forces of aggressive Arab nationalism represented particularly by the United Arab Republic. The large Moslem population in many West African states does not appear to prejudice the latter against Israel's assistance, but it makes U.A.R. penetration that much easier. The U.A.R., however, is not able to offer the services and the skills to tropical Africa that Israel is lending with great success.

In pursuing its commercial and diplomatic policies, Israel has the advantage of being not part of the Soviet world and yet not a great Western power either. It is a partially underdeveloped country many of whose economic problems, especially agricultural, have had a strong resemblance to those of some of the subsaharan states. It is new, dynamic and tough; and it has technical skills it is willing and eager to share with the formerly colonial countries. Israel has been able to help Ghana in industrial and agricultural projects; Israel and Ghana created a jointly-owned shipping line (now owned wholly by Ghana); an Israeli construction group has undertaken important public works in Ghana; Israel is training both merchant marine and air force. Reputedly the best-informed and most influential diplomat in Accra was for a considerable period the ambassador from Israel. Despite this close relationship with Israel, Nkrumah joined the four other most radical of the independent African states at the Casablanca conference in early 1961 to denounce Israel, at Nasser's demand, as an "instrument of imperialism and neo-colonialism." Neither Nkrumah nor Mobido Keita of Mali, who also has close relations with Israel, could possibly have believed this statement that they signed in order to preserve apparent harmony with Nasser.

Unlike many parts of Africa, Ghana has a long tradition of contact with the West. Portuguese, Swedes, Dutch, Danes and finally the British all touched the Gold Coast through the centuries, and all left their mark. Coal-black descendants of Danish Jews who came to Accra well over a century ago still live in the houses of their ancestors. There is a majestic castle on a headland over the ocean, long the symbol of colonial authority and now a residence for Nkrumah. There is an ex-Dutch fort and an ex-Danish fort and an ex-British fort, overlooking the last great surf harbor in West Africa, where freight is unloaded from ships at anchor in the roadstead onto long, thin canoes that the surf boys skillfully maneuver across the waves and up the beach. A few miles away the most modern harbor on the coast is now being built; and, for all its authoritarianism, it took the government many months to succeed in evicting the resident fishermen from the site so construction could begin.

In the cluttered offices of the capital, crisp English civil servants sit next to cabinet ministers dressed in brilliantly colored togas. Ghana has English-style law and currency, the ballot is secret, and traffic moves to the left. Corruption in government is common (a 6 to 10 per cent "cut" on every contract is normal); but the courts are remarkably independent. Accra is a kaleidoscope of color, of activity, of drive and of dirt. In its midst is a fetid swamp that can't be drained because of the god who lives in it; but the city has a "skyscraper" or two, and one of the best hotels in Africa—government-owned. People still die in Accra of starvation. Nowhere is the contrast greater, not even in Nigeria, between Africa emergent and Africa of the primitive bush.

If Nkrumah's dream is for pan-Africa, a union of African states, it does not seem likely of realization in the near future. His first step toward achieving it, a link with French-speaking Guinea, is still more nominal than real; and his second step, a legislative union with French-speaking Mali, is still undefined. His relations with his nearest neighbors to the west and east are particularly cool. On the west, Nkrumah mistrusts the leader of the Ivory Coast, Houphouet Boigny, because in the past the latter has been so closely tied to France; in the east, he is at serious odds with his neighbor, Premier Sylvanus Olympio of Togoland, whose Ewe population Nkrumah would like to include within Ghana's too-confining borders.

The build-up in arms to which Nkrumah has devoted some of Ghana's resources has an ugly look. It is too soon to say whether his pan-Africanism may yet be turned into a form of neo-imperialism; but Nkrumah's tendency to expand his state and his power are no more reassuring than his desire to interfere in the Congo with an exclusively African force.

The Ghanaian outlook on international politics is, as one Western diplomat put it, "not ideological, but practical." While following a foreign policy described as "positive neutralism," Nkrumah has been considered in the past by those who know him as essentially pro-Western. But the course of Ghana's words and actions has recently been moving in the opposite direction, and the influence of the most important of the British ex-civil servants who had stayed on in government employ has clearly declined.

Both Nkrumah's speeches and Ghana's votes in the U.N. reflected this change in attitude, and tended increasingly to coincide with the Soviet-bloc position, most spectacularly in the dispute over the Congo. But it would be erroneous to jump to the conclusion that Ghana was following a Soviet line. It would be much more accurate to say that Ghana was following a policy of shortsighted self-interest that paralleled the Soviet line. To most Ghanaians, it is still the West, not the U.S.S.R., that stands for colonialism; and telling them to beware of Communism is, as one observer put it, like "telling a man in a burning house not to go outside because it may start to snow."

Nkrumah's support of Lumumba in the Congo was based on his hope of stamping out Western—especially Belgian—influence there. He had no desire to see Soviet colonialism substituted for it; but he ignored this risk in the determined effort to prevent any possible return of Belgian control via the more moderate Congolese leaders who were Lumumba's enemies.

Nkrumah's reasons for backing Lumumba were numerous. Lumumba had begun his meteoric rise to political power after attending an African "People's Conference" in Accra only a few years earlier. More than any other Congolese politician, he could be considered Nkrumah's "man." More importantly, Lumumba represented in the Congo the principle of centralism that Nkrumah represented in Ghana. Lumumba was not a strictly tribal leader, as were Kasavubu, Tshombé, Kalonji and the rest. For all his demagogy and instability he was the nearest thing to a native national leader the Congo had; he alone represented a threat to the power of the tribal and regional chiefs. If the Congo were to become a unitary state like Ghana, it would suit Nkrumah's interest that it do so under Lumumba, already a friend of Ghana.

Furthermore, Nkrumah supported Lumumba, as did a number of other African leaders, on the ground of legitimacy—a strange word to come approvingly from revolutionists. It could be, and was, argued that Lumumba had at one point been legally named Premier. If he could be overthrown by internal military force with international acquiescence, the same thing might happen to any other African head of government. None, including Nkrumah, feels yet secure. The subsequent murder of Lumumba while he was prisoner of the separatist government of Katanga could only intensify these feelings of Nkrumah and like-minded African leaders.

There was one further and important consideration for Nkrumah in the Congo. That was the advent of Nigeria. If Nkrumah could help to establish a strongly centralized and friendly Congo, he would have gone far toward building a powerful counterweight on the West Coast of Africa to the one huge new state that vastly overshadows Ghana in size and threatens to overshadow it in prestige. That state is Nigeria, whose population, largest on the African Continent, is some six times that of little Ghana.

CHAPTER **6**

Dirt and Dynamism: Nigeria

Adeniji Adela II is Oba of Lagos. He is titular ruler of the capital of Nigeria, surely one of the dirtiest, ugliest, noisiest, most crowded, and yet liveliest, gayest, most vibrant cities of all West Africa. Its open markets glow with color: row after row of bright blue bolts of cloth; platters full of red peppers and green leaves; mounds of white salt; piles of glistening copper or aluminum pots and pans; bleating herds of brown goats; and through and around the stalls, a ceaseless movement of tall black men in multi-hued robes; handsome women carrying immense burdens of vegetables, or tins, or furniture, or sticks, or laundry, or baskets full of clucking chickens on their heads and contented babies on their backs; ragged children scurrying to and fro beneath the feet of passers-by—everyone going somewhere and in a hurry.

The Oba of Lagos sits in his yellow-stucco tumbledown house, where the dusty "throne room" with its sticks of ancient furniture is decorated with old photographs of British and Nigerian notables, including Queen Elizabeth, Prince Philip and the Oba of Lagos. Above the mid-Victorian chair that serves as a throne there are painted the two words: "The Palace." The Oba, a leather-faced anachronism clad all in white, exercises his minimal powers in solemn conclave with his council of a dozen men and women in

49

the antechamber of the "throne room." They sprawl on the floor beneath his feet as he sits on a dais, talking sometimes to them and sometimes into a telephone, the one touch of the twentieth century in sight.

The Oba and the many other chiefs with equally romantic titles who are scattered throughout Nigeria are on the way out in this federated parliamentary democracy that has been better prepared than most new countries to assume the responsibilities of independence. Half the size of Western Europe, Nigeria with its 35 million inhabitants is the most populous nation on the African Continent, and is destined to become one of the most important. If it includes a feudal society in the Moslem north, it includes a progressive social-welfare state in the west. If it is medieval enough to have obas and emirs and onis and alakes and other kinds of tribal chieftains living in mud-walled palaces reminiscent of *Beau Geste,* it is modern enough to have a political campaign in which one of the principal contestants (himself a chief) swooped down on rallies in the bush in his private helicopter. If it has witch doctors in every village and juju stalls in every market, it has a magnificent ultramodern university with a thousand students (practically all Nigerian), working toward degrees that are based on the standards of the University of London.

If British-born civil servants still abound throughout this country, especially in the northern half, the process of "Nigerianization" is being pushed by a special Nigerianization Office headed by a Nigerian Cambridge graduate. In the top group of civil servants the ratio of Nigerians to Europeans is already one to six. The higher judiciary is at least one-third African and the lower practically all Nigerian. The Chief Justice, a Nigerian, sits in his red robe and white wig in a decorous court that—except for the color of the skin of most of its occupants—would be appropriate in the capital of the Commonwealth to which Nigeria belongs. Yet even now, when over 50 per cent of the children of primary school age attend some kind of classes, less than 1 per cent of those of high school age are receiving secondary education. Nigeria needs two thousand college graduates a year to maintain its present rate of growth; it produces only four hundred men and women eligible to enter universities. Only one-tenth of 1 per cent of Nigeria's population fits into the crucial category of high-level manpower—broadly speaking, professional and technical personnel—compared with 3 or 4 per cent in advanced societies such as the United States or the Soviet Union.

If there are less than a thousand physicians in the entire country, there is a plan (drawn up by a group of British, American and Nigerian experts in 1960 under chairmanship of Sir Eric Ashby) that would vastly expand the entire educational system from primary school through college, provide for establishment of two new universities, and train thousands of doctors, engineers and other specialists. Fortunately, leading Nigerians realize that the basic problem of their country is less lack of investment than lack of trained manpower; and they know, as the Ashby report states, that "factories and power stations can be built in three or four years but to educate the men who will manage them takes twenty."

Nigeria's sophisticated politicians view with amused disdain the efforts of leaders in other and smaller West African countries to carry the torch for a united Africa. "Why should we worry about Ghana assuming leadership of a pan-African movement?" they ask. "All of Ghana isn't even as big as one province of Nigeria."

This huge federation's political evolution under British guidance has been relatively peaceful, facilitated by the wise policy of the colonial administrators forbidding white settlers from establishing themselves on the land. There is no "colon" problem in British West Africa, as there is in British East, or in Algeria to the north; and there is no color problem either.

The antagonisms in Nigeria are now less between black and white than between black and black. Nigeria is divided into four parts: the huge north, mainly Moslem; the relatively progressive west, largely inhabited by the Yoruba tribe; the east, home of the energetic Ibos; and Lagos, the capital. Each of the three provinces has its own government with its own premier, each dominated by a political party representing the major tribal or religious group. The tribal, religious and regional pulls are strong; but as education and urbanization proceed, Nigeria is painfully becoming a nation.

The last elections, in December, 1959, were carried out with remarkable order—all the more remarkable in the light of the hysterical violence of the party press. The campaign was fought more on the basis of tribalism, regionalism, religion and personalities than on substantial political issues; and the three-way division of the country was clearly reflected in the results. The conservative Moslems of the north—where only men were allowed to vote, in contrast to universal suffrage elsewhere in the country—gave to the Federal legislature a plurality of Moslem party members, reflecting the numerical superiority of the Moslems in the Nigerian electorate.

The foreign policy of the Prime Minister, Sir Abubakar Tafawa Balewa, is one of sticking with "our known and proved friends," meaning the British, tempered by the maintenance of close religious ties with the Moslems of Northern Africa and by a growing tendency toward neutralism in the votes at the United Nations. Still, Nigeria and Britain have a defense pact, providing for the training of Nigerian soldiers, sailors and airmen in Britain. And, despite her Moslem majority, Nigeria has increasingly close diplomatic and commercial relations with Israel.

The leader of the opposition, Chief Awolowo, differs from the normal run of African politicians by wholeheartedly and unequivocally aligning himself with the West on the ground that "Africans who believe in the dignity of human beings would be the losers if Communism should prevail." Awolowo, who until he entered the Federal Parliament had been Premier of the Western Region of Nigeria, is an illustration of the progressive type of political leader that his country is beginning to produce. "I believe in the democratic way of life and in the welfare of the masses—a frankly welfare state," he says in his excellent English. He points to the social advances already accomplished in his Western Region—far in advance of anywhere else in Nigeria. Free primary education; free medical treatment for all between the ages of one and eighteen; a system of agricultural loans; experiments in large-scale farming; encouragement of co-operatives on the Israeli model; a housing-construction fund; television (just introduced to Nigeria) in the schools—these are indicators of the way progressive local politicians are thinking.

All of this goes on in a nation containing nearly 250 tribal and linguistic groups, where there are only 18,000 whites in a population of 35 million (1/20 per cent, the smallest proportion of any major African country); where the national income is less than ninety dollars a year; where a few days before an eclipse of the sun the government placed a reassuring advertisement in the newspapers stating, "There is nothing to fear from . . . the darkness"; where "star and occult work" is advertised next to the latest in English literature; where corruption and nepotism are common, but so is an idealistic determination that this new and greatest of African states will succeed.

To help it succeed, the British started Nigeria off in its independence with a $33.6-million loan. Nigeria already had (1958) over $800 million in export and import trade, larger than that of any other country between the Sahara and the Union. The exports are 85 per cent agricultural, primarily in palm kernels and palm oil, of which Nigeria is the world's largest producer, and peanuts and cocoa. Nigeria's gross national income (but not its per capita income) is the largest of any Central African state, exceeding that of the Rhodesias and British East Africa combined.

Not much time will be wasted in Nigeria on political pan-Africanism. "It's a fine ideal but it isn't practicable now," says one leading politician. "You don't find Mac and Jack wasting time sitting around discussing world government, do you? Well, a pan-African state is equally impracticable for us. Economic and social co-operation with our neighboring countries makes more sense. Nkrumah thinks the best way for him to demonstrate his greatness is by being President of a United Africa; I'd rather become great by raising the standard of living of my own country."

CHAPTER 7

Cornucopia of Tension: Cameroon

Progress of the subsaharan African states toward independence has been relatively smooth along the West Coast, unhindered as they were by the problems of major white settlement and assisted— particularly in the case of the British possessions—by an increasingly helpful attitude of the colonial power in preparing them for the burden of self-government. But as one moves out of West and into Equatorial Africa, some of the newly independent countries present a different and more forbidding aspect.

Cameroon, that huge cornucopia that spills down from the desert regions of the Sahara to the tropical coastal forests in the curve of the Gulf of Guinea, achieved its official freedom on the first day of 1960. The first U.N. trust territory to gain its independence, Cameroon had been under effective French control since the end of World War I, when it was taken over from the Germans. It is now formally on its own; but the infancy of its independence has been marked by spasmodic murder and brigandage that have kept the country in a state of alarm for the last few years.

The tension is sensed by the arriving traveler as soon as he steps out of his plane at the airport of Douala, principal city of Cameroon.

54

As dusk falls, soldiers move about, taking up positions. The customs inspector comments, "Things aren't going well." An air of nervousness permeates the atmosphere—reminiscent of Cyprus a few years ago at the height of the terror. "This is the dangerous hour," someone says, "between sunset and the curfew. This is when they make their raids." Precisely at 10 P.M. the gates of the hotel in the center of town clang shut and the guests peer out at deserted streets, the darkness stabbed occasionally by lights of a wandering patrol.

Who are "they"—the terrorists that have occasionally swooped into Douala or the muddy, rain-drenched capital of Yaoundé, a few hundred miles up in the hills? They are, according to the government, brigands and bandits; but according to their leaders, they are fighters for the liberation of Cameroon from French domination.

But as the country is now completely free, why the fight for "independence"? The answer, given in a torrent of words by the late Dr. Felix Moumié, the exiled "rebel" leader who received sanctuary and encouragement in Conakry, was that Premier Ahidjo of Cameroon was but a French puppet and his government no more independent of France now than before the termination of trusteeship.

Terrorism began in 1953 when a leftist party, Union of the Cameroon People (UPC), took up arms for independence against the French. Guerrilla warfare went on sporadically for years, during which an election was held that the UPC boycotted on the grounds that it was rigged. The fighting finally died down, some of the rebel leaders returned to peaceful political activity while others (including Moumié) went into exile; and this huge country of only three million people prepared for an end of the French trusteeship under Premier Ahidjo.

The exiles, however, demanded that prior to independence a new election be held under U.N. supervision; but the proposal was rejected. Terrorism broke out again in the summer of 1959, and has continued intermittently. It is partly political, inspired by such pro-Communist leaders as Moumié was; but it also springs in part from deep-seated social and tribal unrest, especially in the western regions. In this area, a hilly and relatively temperate zone, where the Bamiléké tribe is concentrated, the guerrilla warfare has sometimes reached battle proportions. In June, 1960, for example, over two hundred rebels were killed in an operation by Cameroonian "security forces." But since then, things have quieted down.

Without the continued presence of French troops in Cameroon, Ahidjo's government might not have been able to halt the terrorism. At the third conference of independent African states at Addis Abada in 1960, the Guineans demanded withdrawal of all foreign troops from Africa, specifically the French from Cameroon. The Foreign Minister of Cameroon, Charles Okala, retorted that Guinea was "loading the Cameroon with Czechoslovak arms." There can be no doubt at all that Guinea has consistently attempted to subvert the Ahidjo government on the grounds that it is a tool of France. It was from Guinea and Cairo that the late Dr. Moumié operated, and it was from these centers that he was able to visit Moscow and Peiping to gain financial and possibly military help for the rebels. On the last such trip, he stopped off in Geneva, only to be administered a fatal dose of rat poison by an unknown hand, allegedly that of a secret French counter-terrorist organization.

No country in Africa is more deeply affected by the normal tribal and regional differences than is Cameroon. Containing some eighty different tribes, it is known as the "racial crossroads" of the continent. As in Nigeria, the northern half is dominated by a Moslem conservative ruling class; the southwestern coastal region is non-Moslem, progressive and—for subsaharan Africa—surprisingly literate. It is estimated that 92 per cent of the children in the south get primary schooling, compared with 38 per cent in the north. Also, as in Nigeria, the conservative northern chieftains are more dependent on European advisers than are the southerners. Just prior to independence, three-fourths of the southern prefectures were being administered by Cameroonians; but the French were still dominant in the administration in the north. The Premier himself, a Moslem from the north, is friendly to the French and leans heavily on French advice—which, of course, is the major point of attack on the part of his political enemies both within and without the country.

Ahidjo is Cameroon's strong man, the only political leader who can hold the country together even as well as it is being held with its eighty-four legally constituted "political parties." In the February, 1960, referendum on the new constitution, the adverse vote was high—the constitution being approved only by 800,000 pro to 530,000 con. Yet Ahidjo felt strong enough to remove the old French-imposed ban on the UPC, his most powerful opposition; and two months later he held a general election, in which his party received almost half the total number of votes (mostly from the Moslem north). The fact that nearly 70 per cent of the eligible voters participated in this election suggests that the dissidents may now be turning to the weapon of the ballot box and away from the fruitless terrorism that has racked Cameroon so long.

Ahidjo does not believe that Cameroon should become a "strictly parliamentary" regime, and he has said so. The conditions of internal unrest and external pressures are going to require a strong government and, if it is to survive, a centralized one. If it is to survive— that is the question in Cameroon. It is a country with even less natural unity than most, a country where the average unskilled wage is twenty-five dollars a month, a country with perhaps fifty trained African medical practitioners for the entire population, a country that needs French help to pay for the army it must have, a country that requires—and will require—continued international support if it is not to fall apart.

The economy of Cameroon (except for the port of Douala) is almost entirely dependent on agriculture. Cameroon is one of the world's leading cocoa producers but the quality is not too high. It also exports coffee, bananas, rubber and timber, though deforestation and erosion—as in much of Africa—are severe hindrances to the proper exploitation of forest resources. Political unrest in the country, not to mention its unfavorable climatic and health picture, have kept private investment down.

The truth is that despite its forty years of French tutelage (and thirty years of German before that) Cameroon was as badly prepared as any country in Africa for the responsibilities of independence.

Even in the last decade, when the political winds were unmistakable, the French utterly failed to produce an adequate administrative class. It is a country where a high French official could say with cynicism, just prior to independence: "We have a trained and able man in Ahidjo; and in these countries if they have even one such man, that's already not too bad."

CHAPTER 8

The Adolescents: French Africa

If the French left their Cameroon trusteeship in perilous state—due in part to circumstances beyond their control—they did better with most of their other colonies in West and Equatorial Africa. Not that the educational level or the economic development or the political sophistication of any of these states is anything to boast about. But at least they have moved into independence with relative tranquillity and with continuing bonds of attachment to their former mentors. By and large, the states of subsaharan Africa that are still linked to France in the amorphous Communauté are like adolescent children determined to be free of parental control yet absolutely dependent on their parents for sustenance and support.

In the rapid metamorphosis of the French Communauté in 1960, these colonies all insisted on, and were given, their nominal independence. They have acquired control of diplomacy, defense, finances—all previously reserved to the Communauté—but all have chosen to maintain the intimate contact with France and aid from France that are necessary to their survival, for which the only alternative would have been Soviet penetration in the manner of Guinea or Mali. While these French subsaharan states did not follow a consistently "Western" line at their first U.N. session, they tended to hew more closely to the West than did most of the others. And on the crucial Algerian question, they vainly exerted what influence they could toward adoption of a moderate resolution that would have been less unacceptable to France than the one backed by the more outspoken "anticolonial" of the African countries.

In most of the new African states, the desire of the few educated elite to hold important offices and grandiloquent titles has worked along with tribalism and regionalism against the forces of political federation. But the historic grouping of some of the old French colonies into the two huge administrative units called French West Africa and French Equatorial Africa, plus the overriding demands of present economic necessity, have resulted in two new associations among seven of the eight former French colonies stretching from the Ivory Coast to the Congo.

The four West African states of Ivory Coast, Upper Volta, Dahomey and Niger have created a loose organization and customs union within the Communauté called the Council of the Entente. Leader of the four is the Ivory Coast, relatively prosperous with its rapidly developing port of Abidjan and its large export trade in coffee, cocoa and lumber.

Dominating the Ivory Coast is the remarkable planter-physician-politician Felix Houphouet-Boigny. So completely does the franco-phile Houphouet-Boigny control his country that in the 1957 election his party won fifty-eight out of the sixty seats, and three years later took every seat in the National Assembly with over 98 per cent of the popular vote. Houphouet-Boigny has cool relations with both his left-wing neighbors, Ghana and Guinea, on east and west. At least one dissident tribal chieftain on the Ghana border was recently sentenced to jail for ten years and to banishment for twenty—an indication that even in the tightly run Ivory Coast the borders are anything but secure.

Striving to create some kind of unity out of the old French colonies, Houphouet-Boigny is using the Council of the Entente as one base, and the equally loose grouping of three of the four Equatorial African states—Congo, Central African Republic and Chad—as another (dubbed the Union of Central Africa). The fourth of the Equatorial republics, Gabon, has remained fairly aloof from the others because it is potentially so much wealthier than they, with its oil, its timber resources and with its iron and manganese deposits that are among the richest known to man. All these states are strongly oriented to France, as illustrated by the words of Leon M'ba, Premier of Gabon, who at the moment he received his country's independence in the summer of 1960 turned to the French Premier Michel Debré and said: "You can count on Gabon's remaining with France for better or for worse."

Perhaps the most familiar to the outside world of all these countries is the Congo Republic, because it was in its present capital of Brazzaville that General de Gaulle established the headquarters of Free France for a while during the Second World War. Brazzaville and the Congo are now presided over by a former priest who still wears his robes, the "Abbé" Fulbert Youlou, as astute and tough a politician as ever came up out of Tammany. As usual, the rival parties in Congo represent rival ethnic groupings, which now manage to get along in relative peace since the bloody intertribal outbreak of 1959 that cost more than one hundred lives before it was put down by French troops. After this fracas, Youlou ensured his success at the polls by jailing his principal opponent and gerrymandering the districts in the best professional manner. In the subsequent election his party received 64 per cent of the popular vote, but managed to capture 84 per cent of the seats in the legislative assembly. Youlou's government was not very strong in administrative experience. One of its African members had allegedly served a jail term for practicing slavery, and another, it was said, grew up to manhood as a cannibal. In any event, a government was formed and has managed to function ever since, with support of French "*fonctionnaires*" or civil servants, still carrying on their duties almost as in the days prior to independence.

"The Africans want us to stay on to help them," a high-ranking Frenchman in Brazzaville commented, "but they reserve the administrative jobs for themselves." Frequently a French adviser sits in with a cabinet minister, and guides him not only in his decisions but even in his statements—a true alter ego without whom the governmental work could hardly be performed. At the time of independence in the Congo, close to 80 per cent of all the *"fonctionnaires"* (except schoolteachers) were still French.

"We are trying to establish new schools for higher education," one African official observed, "because too many of our Congolese students who have gone to Paris to finish their studies have come back with Communist ideas." Communist penetration in the Congo and in the other French Equatorial states is as yet almost nil; and the prevailing temper of the Africans in charge is to keep it that way. For instance, a cabinet officer observed: "We don't want aid through the U.N. We prefer direct aid from France and the Western countries, for in that way we avoid danger of Russian 'technicians' such as arrived in the Belgian Congo immediately after independence." This is not the prevailing view in tropical Africa; in fact, the contrary is true. But it is illustrative of the thinking in some of the old French colonies.

The Congo's trade balance is heavily unfavorable, its only important export being tropical woods. "I can't say we're really independent as long as we haven't a strong economy," Youlou asserts; and to build that economy he hopes to attract enough capital to construct a huge dam in the gorge of the Kouilou, which reputedly would produce the cheapest hydroelectric power in all of Africa—if it could find a market, possibly in mineral development of neighboring Gabon.

Brazzaville itself, surmounted by a modern 750-bed hospital that symbolizes the benevolent side of French colonialism in the Congo, is a hot and humid town of nondescript buildings sprawled along the right bank of the great river that has given its name to the two republics on either side. "Brazza's" twin is "Léo" (Léopoldville); and the two face each other across the muddy Congo at the point above the rapids where navigation begins up that mighty stream for a thousand miles into the heart of Central Africa. "Twin" only because of their location, the two capitals bear little resemblance to each other physically and less psychologically.

In Brazzaville, half-clad African women cluster gaily around the water pumps, to bathe their myriad children, to gossip, and to nod and smile at any occasional European passer-by. Even when they object to having their pictures taken, they do it with a laugh, running behind the nearest tree amid screams of joy as though they were playing a game of tag.

Across the river in Léopoldville, with its broad boulevards and modern skyscrapers, things were visibly different even before independence. In the native district, one instantly felt an atmosphere of sullen truculence tinged with hostility directed against any European (white) intruder. No smiles, no nods, no friendly gestures. In gay and casual Brazzaville, two whites entering a café in the native quarter of "Poto-Poto" are offered a drink by a neighboring party of Africans. It is hard to imagine such a thing happening in Léopoldville at any time. After July 1, 1960, it was of course unthinkable.

CHAPTER 9

The Magic Box: Congo

A magic potion in a little black box called "independence" was sold early in the summer of 1960 in the villages of the Congo with a warning tag: "Do not Open Until June 30." On the mystic day, those who had bought the boxes and expected miracles found only rocks inside. The purpose of the sharpers who had cheated them was fraudulent; but their action was more symbolic than they knew.

On June 30 the 13½ million people of the Belgian Congo collectively opened their magic box. Its name was "independence"; and there was only rock inside. There was no potion for creating, fullblown, a viable state; no formula for guaranteeing the unalienable rights of life, liberty and the pursuit of happiness; no alchemy to assure freedom for the individual or stability for the government in the face of the massive unpreparedness of this once imperial domain.

The vast expanse of the Congo, about one-fourth the area of the United States, was almost totally unready for the independence that its few articulate leaders demanded, that its inarticulate people supported, and that its Belgian rulers suddenly yielded with more haste than courage. Hardly five years ago, a renowned American observer could write: "The Congo is in many ways a refreshing place. The Belgians make no bones about it. Theirs is a colony ruled by Belgians—by Belgians from Belgium. Nobody votes, not even the Belgians who live there."

It was even more recently that the very first elections ever to take place in the Belgian Congo were held, and then in just three communities. The first nationwide elections came late in 1959, and these were but for local councils. Six months later, the Republic of the Congo was a sovereign state. What had happened to cause this extraordinary, pell-mell rush to independence?

With its great mineral wealth in copper, cobalt and uranium (concentrated in the southeastern province of Katanga) and with a relatively high standard of living for the African labor force, the Congo had long seemed to virtually all observers a stable, tightly run, profitable and entirely paternalistic colonial domain. The per capita income was low—at the normal level for tropical Africa of far less than one hundred dollars per year—but the share of the Congolese in the total income had been rising; the balance of trade favorable and the budget in equilibrium until recently; and the social and economic works of the Belgians considerable.

But the winds of freedom sweeping over Africa blew with especial strength from the French side of the broad Congo River that separates the former Belgian from the former French possessions. Political stirrings were taking place in French Equatorial Africa, particularly evident after the Congo Republic was declared an autonomous unit of the French Communauté in December, 1958.

The growing industrialization of the Congo based on its mineral wealth had already resulted in a large-scale detribalization of the natives. Some four million—almost a third—of the entire African population of the country had come to live in cities and their surrounding areas, where they began to feel the restlessness that urbanization, unemployment and sudden dependence on a money economy bring about. Equal pay for equal work became the first cry of the Congolese laborer; from this it was a quick and easy step to agitation for the franchise—even in a country where many tribes have the words neither for "ballot" nor for "voting" in their language.

The Belgians went blindly on in their paternalistic way, building impressive hospitals, enhancing social services, and constructing a huge palace for the Governor General in a fine residential section of Léopoldville on a bluff overlooking the river. "That palace," scoffed a French observer toward the end of '59, pointing to it from the Brazzaville side, "they don't know it yet, but they're building that for Kasavubu." His prediction came true sooner than he—or anyone else—thought possible.

So little had the Belgians prepared their Congolese for self-government—so little had they thought it necessary—that of the fourteen hundred top civil servants, not more than half a dozen were Africans. Although bare literacy is estimated at around 50 per cent, real political and intellectual development for Africans had been almost totally neglected, and so had economic development above a certain level. At the present time in all the Congo, African university graduates number certainly not more than fifty, except those trained for the priesthood. Two universities had been founded in the last few years, but there is only one member of Parliament with an academic degree. There are virtually no professional men, no entrepreneurs, no middle class among the Congolese. The highest governmental jobs held by Africans were almost without exception clerical or lower. The technical jobs needed for any modern economy were almost completely in white hands.

The Belgians thought that their kind of paternalism, often held up as a model of how to run an African state, would be enough. They were hopelessly wrong. Throughout 1958 and 1959 their belated offers of an increasing share in government were unable to keep pace with the demands of the rising leaders of the innumerable party groupings that suddenly sprang up, nourished by the nationalist movements that were exploding all over the rest of tropical Africa. "The trouble is they're plunging into political life without any base or background," commented one American official. "This place was like the Congo above the falls—a smoothly flowing, placid river —until all of a sudden we've come to the rapids, and now nobody knows where we are."

When the Belgians capitulated with a speed that must have surprised even themselves—panicked is the more accurate word for what they did—they handed over independence with all its burdens of political responsibility to a Congo that, like a restlessly sleeping giant, was thrashing about in semi-consciousness, grasping for something in a nightmare without really comprehending what it was.

The Congo was unprepared not only because none of its people had had any training in government. It was also psychologically unprepared. Detribalization has proceeded further than in any other country of tropical Africa, but the dawning political consciousness in the Congo is still to very large degree based on tribal divisions and tribal loyalties. This is the heart of the nationalist dilemma in the Congo as in virtually every other tropical African state. The leading tribes desire self-expression and self-rule, which is obviously at cross purposes with the drive for a truly national unitary government. It takes either a strong leader, as in Ghana (which is much smaller in area and in population, and therefore easier to manage, than the Congo), to cope with tribal separatism; or a strong people as in Nigeria, with more training in self-government than the Congolese were fortunate enough to have.

Added to the problem of tribal rivalries was a widespread hatred of the whites that seemed to run deeper here than anywhere else on the western side of Africa, partly because the proportion of whites in the Congo (about 1 to 125) was greater than in most other places on the West Coast, and partly because of memories running all the way back to the turn of the century, when the Congo was the personal property of Leopold II and the atrocities committed against the natives on the rubber plantations cut deep into the African soul.

Serious as may be the outbursts of Congolese resentment against the whites now that the Congo has its independence, even more serious is the internal division of the country—the hostility of African against African. This goes back many centuries beyond the relatively brief contact of African with European. The Congo embraces within its huge area some two hundred tribes, speaking some four hundred recognizable dialects.

In the hectic months before independence, one of the principal points of discussion both in Léopoldville and in Brussels concerned the degree to which the Congo should be a unitary, as distinct from a federal, state. The first Prime Minister, Patrice Lumumba, was the principal spokesman for a strong central government. His rival, Joseph Kasavubu, was until he became Chief of State far more interested in a loose federation. Why? The main tribe of the southern Congo, the Bakongo, whose leader is Kasavubu, would like to re-create an ancient kingdom of its own stretching all the way from Portuguese Angola, through the lower Congo, and across the river into the former French territory of the Congo Republic. Kasavubu, smiling through his sharply filed teeth, predicted long before independence: "A closely centralized state won't work—it will be like a bundle of faggots tied together; when the string is loosened they fall apart."

Moise Tshombé, Premier of the secessionist province of Katanga, adds: "Let us face the truth. Democracy does not exist here. We have a tribal structure. The last election showed that everybody voted according to tribe." Katanga's secessionist movement stems from genuine political roots, well watered by the Belgian corporation known as UMK, the wealthy Union Minière du Haut Katanga which controls the bulk of the mineral production of the province. Nevertheless, all during the constitutional discussion in Brussels and Léopoldville early in 1960, the Belgians had argued against separatism and in favor of a unitary state, perhaps because they hoped they could more easily control the latter.

Separatist forces have remained strong, and not only in Katanga. In most of the other provincial assemblies, there is fractionalization according to tribe. Just prior to independence, a local minority in five of the Congo's six provinces threatened to set up, in each, a new province based on its tribal strength. "It was tribal warfare," a correspondent observed, "transmuted into political institutions."

This was the problem the United Nations had to face when it embarked on its most daring project for the preservation of international peace since Korea. It is the problem it has to face in the Belgian trust territory of Ruanda-Urundi, which is in a virtually constant state of latent civil war. In the Congo, its duty was to preserve order in concert with the central Congo government, without aiding or hindering the latter in its difficulties with secessionists. It also had the equally difficult task of determining who the central government was, among three or four contenders for the honor, and meanwhile to fend off the power plays of the Soviet Union, of the Belgians, of the U.A.R. and of other African states.

There is no inherent reason why Katanga should belong to the Congo except for the historic accident that King Leopold's domain included it. There is, however, a vital economic reason, and that is that Katanga's mines represent half of the Congo's national wealth. There is an equally important political reason, too. The principle of the unitary state is one that every African ruler supports (with varying degrees of truculence) because each is threatened by disunity within his own borders. Not one of the African states is a genuine tribal, linguistic, ethnic, historic unit; but each leader is determined to create a single nation out of a former colonial domain, and many view the Congo as a test case. As has been pointed out in respect to Ghana, this is a major reason why some supported Lumumba, and still support the ideas he represented.

Out of the welter of cross-currents and conflicting interests, the best solution for the Congo appears to be a federalized state that at once preserves the unitary idea in principle yet leaves to the major tribal groupings a degree of autonomy. Such a compromise might be placed on a firm footing if the Russians, the Egyptians, the Belgians and assorted African states could be persuaded to desist from their interference in the Congo in pursuit of their own purposes.

It was on the fear of separatism (as well as of "Western colonialism") that the Soviet Union played with such success among the Africans in its effort to undermine the U.N.'s position in the Congo. If secession should succeed in the Congo, it might encourage similar movements in Ghana, in Cameroon, or in Nigeria, thereby leading to what the pan-Africanists such as Nkrumah and the most ardent African nationalists call the "Balkanization" of the continent. Their political philosophy points in the opposite direction: toward bigger (not smaller) groupings, in a West African or even an all-African federation.

Paradoxically, secession in the Congo would also encourage separatism in the one place where the African nationalists most ardently desire it: in the still white-dominated Federation of Rhodesia and Nyasaland that lies across the Congo's southeast border.

CHAPTER 10

Another Algeria?——Rhodesia

While white political domination has virtually ended with miraculous speed along the western coast of subsaharan Africa, the European populations have dug in along the continent's eastern spine. In the highlands of Kenya straddling the Equator and in the conglomerate Central African Federation of Rhodesia and Nyasaland, the white settlers have been the immovable object against which the inevitable force of Africanism and anti-colonialism has been crashing with increasing strength. The racial problems on this side of the continent are difficult (in contrast to the other side, where with the exception of the Congo they hardly exist at all), because this is where a few score thousand Europeans have moved in to farm the best land, to operate the rich mines, to build their homes, to live their lives and to cling grimly to a political and economic control that they cannot hope to keep much longer.

Most of them—over 300,000—live in the Federation of Rhodesia and Nyasaland; and the 7.9 million Africans who surround them suffer under greater political, economic and social disabilities than anywhere else except in the neighboring Union of South Africa.

The Federation is one of the weirdest political combinations in all the world, consisting of the self-governing British colony of Southern Rhodesia with the relatively large proportion of 220,000

white settlers to 2.8 million Africans; and the two British protectorates of Northern Rhodesia, with 80,000 Europeans and 2.3 million
Africans, and Nyasaland, with only 9,000 Europeans in an African
population of 2.8 million. These three parts, each with its own
government, have been united since 1953 through the Federation,
which has a top-layer government of its own. Although the "common roll" ballot is used, meaning that Africans and whites vote for
the same candidates, the property and educational qualifications for
voters have been set in such a way as to ensure overwhelming white
supremacy in a land of overwhelming African majorities.

Out of almost 100,000 qualified voters for the Federal election
in 1958, less than 7,000 were Africans. In Southern Rhodesia, where
there has never been an African member of the Legislative Assembly,
there were less than 2,000 African voters out of 68,000; in Nyasaland, with a population ratio of over 300 to 1, there were less than 50
African voters as against 2,000 Europeans. In certain areas of Northern Rhodesia, the extremely complicated voting laws were so fixed
that no matter how many Africans were qualified to vote, the value
of each African ballot could not exceed one-third that of each
European ballot.

The principal opposition to greater African suffrage has come not
from the Colonial Office nor from the wealthier and upper professional classes, but rather from the white artisans, the clerks, the
skilled employees of the "Copper Belt" (many of them from South
Africa), the tradesmen who fear that economic competition from
native Africans will accompany an improved political and educational status. At present the Africans' lack of economic and educational equality matches this lack of political equality. The average
monthly wage for Europeans in the Federation is $265; the Africans'
is $19.

"The differential in wages is justified because of the Africans'
lower productivity," says a Chamber of Commerce official in
Lusaka, Northern Rhodesia's capital, which still has the earmarks
of a pioneer town. "A white bookkeeper is paid about twice what
an African gets, but his output is twice as great." This same
businessman will admit in the same breath that many unqualified

Federation—less than half of one per cent of the total), they are the third party in every East African political crisis. Unfortunately they cannot serve as a bridge between the blacks and whites because they are mutually despised by both, partially for racial and partially for economic reasons. The strong prejudice against them throughout East Africa arises from their reputation as sharp traders, as the middlemen who allegedly exploit both the farmers in the field and the workers in the town.

Despite the lofty buildings and the brisk businessmen who work in them, despite the lovingly tended park where British ladies and gentlemen in immaculate whites play of a Sunday their immaculate game of bowls, despite an absence of night life reminiscent of a British provincial town, Salisbury nevertheless retains its frontier attitudes. Pioneers are still alive who marched with the first wagon train that planted the Union Jack in what is now Southern Rhodesia. The memory of Rhodes and Beit and Jameson is green. The people here talk and look and act like new settlers in a new land, where a favorite phrase is that the native Africans are "but one generation out of the trees."

In all three states of this shaky Federation, change is clearly under way. It may come through a Constitutional reform in Southern Rhodesia, where the proportion of whites is far greater than in the other two parts of the Federation, and the initiative and freedom of the native Africans far less. Even here, where the whites will yield most gradually and least gracefully, concessions were made in the summer of 1960 to assure the election of a small number of Africans to the colony's legislature for the first time in history.

However, it was in Southern Rhodesia that serious strikes and native disturbances during 1960 brought about a panicky repression of moderate African nationalists, the jailing of native leaders and the speedy passage of a "Law and Order Maintenance Act" that the Chief Justice of the Federation said "outrages almost every basic human right."

This law, pushed through by the conservative Southern Rhodesian government of Prime Minister Sir Edgar Whitehead, contained harsh provisions for summary arrest, forcible removal of "vagrants" from one part of the country to another, restrictions on the press and on public gatherings. It was a negative, dead-end response to the Southern Rhodesian Africans' belated demand for more jobs, housing and political emancipation. It is a white man's version of Ghana's notorious Preventive Detention Act; and it can only result in increased bitterness and the widening of the gulf between the Europeans and the Africans of Southern Rhodesia.

Sir Edgar and his controlling United Federal party (which also controls the Federation government under Premier Sir Roy Welensky) are conservative, but not the most conservative voices in Southern Rhodesia and the Federation. They at least pay lip service to the ideal of the multiracial state. To their right is the Dominion party, which is dedicated in fact if not in theory to white rule in the fashion of neighboring South Africa. To achieve this end, the Dominion party would have Southern Rhodesia, plus the "copper belt" area of Northern Rhodesia, form a dominion, i.e., a country even more independent of London than the Federation is already. It is not always realized, in fact, that the legal and actual protector of the Africans in the Federation is the Colonial Office. So far from practicing the stereotype of "colonialism" of which it is traditionally accused, the Colonial Office is in reality a liberal influence on the British settlers in East Africa in their relations with the native peoples. "Our quarrel," the leading African nationalists point out, "is not with the British government but with the white settlers."

The most reactionary of the white settlers in the Dominion party want to rid themselves of any Colonial Office restraints while there is still time and before the Africans assume political control, as they are ultimately sure to do. Some of the whites even envisage Southern Rhodesia's ultimate absorption into the Union of South Africa. There are, of course, many voices of reason in Southern Rhodesia, but the trouble is that there are not enough of them. And if the radical extremists, who believe that repression is the only answer to the rising African demand for representation, maintain control, then there is very serious danger that Southern Rhodesia may yet become another Algeria.

It is to forestall this danger that the white moderates in Salisbury are becoming more outspoken. Among the most outspoken is Sir Ronald Prain, chairman of the Rhodesian Selection Trust, one of the world's greatest copper combines, whose head offices are in Salisbury. Sir Ronald insists that major political and social advances will have to be made, and quickly, in the condition of Africans in the Federation. He has made special note of the need for "urgent and drastic alteration" of the Southern Rhodesian land law, under which over 50 per cent of the land (including most of the best) is reserved for the white population. To change this law would be a drastic change indeed, for Southern Rhodesian tobacco farms and cattle ranches (white-owned) form an important part of a diversified economy, based partly on agriculture, partly on industry and partly on mining wealth in chrome, asbestos and gold.

While political emancipation for the African is slow in Southern Rhodesia, and even seems at times to be retrogressing, it is moving ahead more rapidly in the two other parts of the Federation: Nyasaland and Northern Rhodesia. In Nyasaland, for example, the Colonial Office has already agreed to admit 100,000 Africans to the voting rolls, which will of course mean complete African domination over the white population. In Northern Rhodesia, evolution will not be quite so rapid, partly because the proportion of whites is larger and partly because the vested interests of the Europeans are infinitely greater; for it is here that the copper mines are concentrated, furnishing a third of the Federation's revenue and more than half its export income.

Some Northern Rhodesian whites share these views of a Lusaka politician: "I am not prepared to live in a country under a black government, with a black prime minister, black judges and black policemen, because I don't believe that they have the same high standards of behavior that I am accustomed to. They may reach those standards in time, but there is no sign of it today, as events in other countries [viz., the Congo] have shown."

Nevertheless, already in Northern Rhodesia, segregation in hotels and restaurants is forbidden by law. Already the "color bar" is ending, so far as wages and employment go, in the copper mines. Already Northern Rhodesia has an African or two in the government. Already the influence of the Congo across the border is being powerfully felt. Already many people in Northern Rhodesia are realizing, as one of them has said: "To bring along a few emerged Africans is not enough. We have to bring them all—for as matters stand today, each emerged African is simply a time bomb."

Northern Rhodesia is the home of some outstanding liberals such as Sir John Moffat, leader of the moderate Central African party, exponent of multiracial "partnership." Sir John believes that "a major explosion is inevitable unless prompt action is taken"—the "prompt action" including a large expansion of the African vote and enactment of a constitutional Bill of Rights which would protect Africans from white oppression today, and the whites from African oppression tomorrow.

Most of the African leaders, however, even the moderate ones, have by this time come to reject the "partnership" principle in favor of outright African domination, on the basis that each man (and woman) is entitled to one vote. "Partnership is a sham," says a youthful African politician. "Partnership here means the Europeans always retain control. The European liberals can't be trusted. They've been frightened by rising African power and now want to work with us; but partnership to them is just a device for maintaining white supremacy." This is an accurate enough analysis of the motives of some of the white Rhodesians who talk about "partnership"; but it falls far short of justice to many of those who are striving for a peaceful, orderly way out of a terrible dilemma.

It was in the effort to solve this dilemma that the Monckton Commission in 1960 urged that a real effort be made to work out a truly multiracial society in the Rhodesias. This commission, headed by Lord Monckton and containing British, white Rhodesian and African Rhodesian members, was appointed to examine into the workings of the Federation and come up with recommendations for its constitutional improvement. What the Commission, by overwhelming majority, did was to suggest changes in the organization of the Federation designed to ensure an orderly political evolution rather than racial domination by either whites or blacks. It urged drastic widening of the franchise, an increase of Africans in the Federal Assembly (an equal number of Africans and Europeans), guarantees against racial discrimination (in either direction), a decrease in the functions of the central government and an enlargement of those of the three components, and—the capstone to this proposal—the right to each of eventual secession from the Federation.

This program was too radical for Welensky's ruling party, which does not even wish to consider the possibility of secession. However, it was not radical enough for the African nationalists of Nyasaland and Northern Rhodesia, who do not even wish to consider the possibility of continued federation. They believe that the central government is and will continue to be dominated by the white supremacists of Southern Rhodesia.

They insist on a breakup of the Federation now into its three parts. The Nyasaland leader, Dr. Hastings K. Banda, knows that his impoverished country could not possibly stand alone as an economically viable state; but in his view the first priority is to rid Nyasaland of what is, in effect, Southern Rhodesian control. "Secession now," he says. After that, there may be the possibility of a link with Northern Rhodesia or perhaps with an East African Federation of which Tanganyika and Kenya would form the other principal parts. The Northern Rhodesian nationalists headed by Kenneth Kaunda are equally insistent on severance from the south, and for essentially the same reason.

But the Monckton Commission advised against immediate dissolution in the hope of achieving a workable "partnership" and also in the knowledge that the economic consequences of a breakup would be most serious. The greatest asset of the Federation is Northern Rhodesia's copper (17 per cent of the world's output); and the economy of all three states (Nyasaland supplies labor to the other two) would be thrown gravely off balance if they should each go their separate way. The great Kariba hydroelectric project, now under construction in Southern Rhodesia, will further tie the economy of the whole country together as it produces increasing quantities of cheap power for distribution in both Rhodesias.

The Monckton recommendations are practical and moderate, pointing toward greater political liberty for the blacks and a gradual, dignified retreat for the whites. But it may be that the opportunity for gradualism has already been lost. A genuinely multiracial society—in which the franchise would not be restricted according to color and the votes would be cast according to a candidate's ability, not his race—is the ideal solution in those parts of Africa where the two races live permanently side by side. It already exists in Tanganyika, and it may still have a chance in Kenya. It ought to succeed in a united Rhodesia and possibly it can; but as the extremists on both sides dig in their heels, the prospects become progressively worse, and a breakup of the Federation progressively more probable.

Recommendations such as those of the Monckton Commission could help prevent the Rhodesias from becoming another Congo, or another Union of South Africa, or another Algeria; but the essential element may be missing, and that is statesmanship on the part of both white settlers and black nationalists.

CHAPTER 11

Federation in Embryo: Kenya-Tanganyika

The further up the east side of Africa one travels, the louder are the native voices. In Tanganyika and also in Kenya, scene of the bloody Mau Mau uprising, the color bar is crumbling more quickly, and native politics is more advanced, than in the Federation. Black men are seen as guests in Nairobi's best hotels; and, sure sign of segregation's ultimate collapse, an Asiatic Moslem has been admitted to the Polo Club.

While in Northern and Southern Rhodesia together there are some 300,000 whites to 5.1 million Africans, or a ratio of 1 to 17, the figures for Kenya are quite different. There the white settlers number but 65,000 in a total population of 6 million—or a ratio of about 1 to 100. As in Rhodesia, the whites in Kenya, few as they are, have to a large degree come to stay—in a sense almost unknown on the West Coast of Africa. Together with the 200,000 Asians and Arabs, they form the real economy of Kenya. A few thousands are settled in a region of fertile green farms in a healthy, temperate climate—an area known as the "white highlands," which was wilderness only a generation or two ago, and now accounts for virtually all of Kenya's agricultural production of cattle, coffee and tea. Parts of the "white highlands" are as green as England, with a considerably gentler climate; the cattle are sleek, in striking contrast to the mangy beasts that are a sign of wealth among the African tribes. One can find sizable manor houses reminiscent of those in the Cotswolds, surrounded by luxuriant flower gardens that bring England that much closer. Such a house is inhabited by Michael Blundell, leading European moderate, who came out from Yorkshire in the twenties and has made his fortune in Kenya's fertile hills.

Blundell has long recognized the inevitability of "a transfer of responsibility" to the Africans because of their overwhelming numbers; but he has wanted to accomplish it slowly, by gradually enlarging the franchise and stressing the "partnership" principle—in the hope that Africans might become accustomed to voting for candidates according to merit and not by race. But the Europeans of Kenya have split bitterly under the stress of rising African pressures.

Rejecting Blundell's moderate approach, a coalition of "white settlers" has been formed under Sir Ferdinand Cavendish-Bentinck, former Speaker of the Legislative Council. He accused the Colonial Office of betraying the Europeans' interests in Kenya at the Constitutional Conference held in London in 1960, when the British government recognized the inevitable with characteristic perception. The franchise then was widened enough to ensure at the next election an all-African government. Although the extreme African demands of independence and universal suffrage (one man, one vote) were not met, the balance of power was unmistakably and irretrievably shifted from Europeans to Africans, thus making Kenya the first of the British African territories with an important, permanent white minority to come—as it surely will very soon—under completely black control.

These concessions are far too great for the majority of Europeans, many of whom would stand stubbornly firm as the Southern Rhodesians have done. They are more to the liking of the small liberal group, one of whose members commented ruefully: "When we were advocating political multiracialism a few years ago, actually urging that Africans be given an important stake in the franchise, we were daringly liberal. Now it's hard to find an African whom we can interest in our gradualistic approach, for we're considered far too conservative."

He is right. The concessions were not great enough for many of the leading Africans, including Tom Mboya, general secretary of the Kenya African National Union. A dynamic young trade-unionist, Mboya had seized the ball of Kenya nationalism after the veteran Jomo Kenyatta was exiled to northern Kenya nearly a decade ago for alleged leadership of the Mau Mau rebellion. In Nairobi, Mboya presents a tougher front than he does in New York or Washington. As his penetrating almond eyes burn through the narrow slits of an impassive face relieved only by gleaming white teeth, Mboya asks: "Why should we wait? People aren't in test tubes, to develop by stages. We want democratic rights, without qualification." What he got in London was the promise of a franchise broad enough to ensure African control of the Legislative Council, but with built-in safeguards for the European and Asiatic minorities, and at least a brake on expropriation of lands now reserved to Europeans in the "white highlands."

An end to such reserved status (covering one-fifth of the country's total arable land, and by far the best part of it) is one of Mboya's principal aims: "We want the Europeans to have exactly the same rights as the Africans—no more, no less. It will not be enough just to give the Africans of Kenya equal access to the twelve thousand square miles of the 'white highlands.' We have to make sure that they actually get some of those lands even if that means breaking up the larger European estates and limiting the size of individual holdings. The Europeans have to recognize that the economic situation is bound to change; and when we Africans gain control there will be readjustments of economic power. European rights and interests will be respected; but the unbalanced proportions will have to be reversed: after all, there are one hundred Africans here to every European."

Mboya has no time or patience for multiracialism; he envisages a socialist, welfare-oriented, African state. As is true of most of the nationalist leaders, Mboya represents centralism as against the centrifugal power of the ancient tribal chiefs. A Luo, he has the special disadvantage of not belonging to the country's principal tribe, the Kikuyu. The Luo and Kikuyu together, accounting for almost half of Kenya's population, are allied in his African National Union, while a number of smaller tribes (including the nomadic, cattle-raising "warrior" Masai) are joined in a rival Kenya African Democratic Union under Ronald Ngala, an African who had already reached ministerial status as Minister of Labor.

One of Mboya's closest Kikuyu associates is Dr. Gikonyo Kiano, California-educated Minister of Commerce in the Kenya government. Kiano insists that the Kenya independence movement can succeed despite the scarcity of educated and trained African administrators. "We'd rather make our own mistakes under our own government—and anyway we'd continue to use British civil servants where necessary, as they do in Ghana. We're for 'one man, one vote'; and we'll employ every measure short of violence to attain that end. I've told my people, no more violence, we can't afford it. I want to improve our standard of living; and violence doesn't result in that."

So much has already been yielded to African demands that new violence now seems unlikely in Kenya—far less likely, for example, than in the Rhodesias. Kenya has had its violence, the bloody Mau Mau uprising in which the Kikuyu were principally involved. The Mau Mau episode resulted in the death of about a hundred whites and Asiatics, and of some thirteen thousand Africans, the latter unevenly divided between those who were killed because they did not participate in the rebellion and those who were killed (the great majority) because they did.

After the Africans gain political control in Kenya, the question remains whether they will be able to preserve democratic government guaranteeing rights for all, including the two main minority groups of Europeans and Asiatics. Mboya recognizes the problem faced by other newly independent governments, such as that of Ghana on the opposite side of the continent. "When people have massed together to gain one exciting goal, independence, it may take some time after they get it to calm down to the normal processes of democracy. And perhaps the opposition doesn't know how to act either. A government may well have to consolidate its position for a while before moving into a really democratic state. But in any case, an African dictatorship—if we have to have that—is a whole lot better than a colonial one!"

Such sentiments are, naturally, not too well received by the Europeans of Kenya, nor the Ismaili Moslems, nor the old-style tribal chieftains. But Mboya's words represent the opinion of the African nationalists who are coming to power in Kenya—whether they come under the leadership of Mboya or one of his several and more extreme rivals.

In contrast to the rejection by most articulate African politicians of multi-racialism in Kenya, is its full and open acceptance by the undisputed leader of Tanganyika, Julius Nyerere. This amazing young man became prime minister of the British trust territory in 1960, after elections had been held under a new franchise that gave to elected Africans a majority of the Legislative Council. Nyerere actually espouses multiracialism in principle and carries it out in political practice. Of the ten ministers he named in 1960, seven are African, two European and one Asiatic. "We in Tanganyika believe that only a wicked man can make color the criterion for rights," he says.

Nyerere is a European-educated ex-schoolmaster in his late thirties, who is head of the Tanganyika African National Union that is the core of the independence movement. "Here we intend to build a country in which the color of a person's skin or the texture of his hair will be as irrelevant to his rights and his duties, as a citizen, as it is irrelevant to his value in the eyes of God."

But Nyerere also points out that the secret of his "moderation" lies in the fact that Tanganyika has very few white settlers; only one-third as many as in Kenya, and proportionately fewer. In Tanganyika there are but 23,000 whites (perhaps 1,200 settled on their own land) plus 112,000 Asiatics, and 9,000,000 Africans.

"We have the Germans to thank for this," Nyerere notes with a smile. "Tanganyika was a German colony until it was given as a mandate to Britain after the First World War. There weren't many

German settlers in the first place; and in the twenties and thirties they stopped coming altogether, and the British went to more attractive places such as Kenya and Rhodesia. Then during the Second World War, many of the Germans were removed—with the result that when self-government and independence got in the air after 1945, the proportion of Europeans in Tanganyika was minute. And the ones who were there were realistic enough to see that more good could be accomplished by working with the Africans than against them. I don't consider myself particularly a 'moderate.' If I were in Kenya, I'd act the way Mboya does; but I had luckier circumstances here in Tanganyika."

The most important factor that makes Nyerere's path easier, aside from the small number of whites, is their ownership of only 1.5 per cent of the total land area of this almost totally agricultural and pastoral country. Nor do they completely dominate it economically. While the large sisal plantations (Tanganyika supplies two-fifths of the world's output of this fiber) are almost wholly European-owned, coffee and cotton production are not, the latter being mainly in African hands. Tanganyika's most important mineral export, diamonds from the famous Williamson mine, is now controlled jointly by the government and de Beers.

One-party rule—which Nyerere will inevitably have when he takes over the reins of government—is not "necessarily undemocratic," he maintains with his ready smile. "Democracy is essentially government by discussion—and nobody can teach Africans how to discuss." One of the things they are sure to discuss under Nyerere's leadership is his favorite idea of an East African Federation that will join Tanganyika, Kenya, the protectorate of Uganda, the tiny colony of Zanzibar and ultimately, it is possible, Nyasaland and Northern Rhodesia as well.

Uganda, slightly smaller in population than Kenya (5.8 million) and with even fewer Europeans and Asians than Tanganyika (9,000 and 57,000 respectively), was at one time considered the most politically advanced of the three states. But the determination of the Cambridge-educated ruler of its biggest and richest province,

Buganda, to maintain his kingdom as an entity separate from the rest of Uganda has slowed progress toward self-government for the country as a whole. No strong leader has yet emerged in the rest of Uganda, which contains more than a dozen principal tribes speaking at least five languages without the unifying influence of Swahili, the lingua franca for Tanganyika and Kenya.

Nevertheless, the movement for an East African Federation is logical and will surely become stronger. As everywhere else in Africa, there would be serious leadership rivalries—among Nyerere of Tanganyika, Kenyatta and Mboya of Kenya, Banda of Nyasaland, Kaunda of Northern Rhodesia, to name only the more prominent African politicians. But there is more common interest, there are more of the elements of unity, here in formerly British East Africa than can be found on the other side of the continent. In contrast to West Africa, where French and English-speaking areas are intermingled, almost all this part of East Africa speaks English, or Swahili, or both. While each country individually is economically weak, together they would be viable, especially if Northern Rhodesia with its enormous mineral wealth were included.

A unified customs department has long existed under control of the East Africa High Commission, which shares with the respective governments responsibility for development of Kenya, Uganda and Tanganyika. Currency in these three states is the same, under control of the East Africa Currency Board, and the rail and port facilities are unified under the East African Railways and Harbors administration. Students from all three countries enter Makerere College in Uganda, the principal institution of higher education (with University of London standards) for East Africa. The three states (plus Zanzibar) would naturally fit into a union even without Nyasaland and Northern Rhodesia. The least that can be said is that Nyerere's dream of federation has on the face of it more validity than Touré's or Nkrumah's.

Part II

CHAPTER 12

The Plastic Curtain: U.S.S.R.

On the Communist fringe of Eastern Europe, as in subsaharan Africa, American policy to be effective can no longer be cast in terms of generalities. On the eastern edge of the Western world, as in Africa, it must be cut to fit different patterns.

The Communist structure of Eastern Europe is neither breaking up nor breaking apart; but it is full of differences in outlook, culture and attitudes so deep and so far-reaching that they become almost tangible as one travels through that area still sometimes mislabeled the "monolithic" empire.

In Europe's sprawling House of Communism, Moscow is the central sanctuary to which the faithful make obeisance, while restiveness is found in Warsaw and dissidence in Belgrade. The blinds on Poland's windows are partly drawn, but behind them are uneasy stirrings; Yugoslavia's shutters are now thrown wide, and the self-conscious vaunting of unorthodoxy is heard within. In evaluating these two parts of Communism's House, it is helpful first to keep in mind the atmosphere of Moscow.

Now boasting five million people, Moscow offers the same impression it must have given a half-century ago when it was the mercantile capital of the czar's domains: a drab city of business without

91

the warmth and personality of cultured Warsaw, or of luminous, water-borne Leningrad, or even of the tree-studded provincial capital of Kiev. The towers of the Kremlin are now dwarfed by seven almost identically ugly skyscrapers scattered about the city like seven upthrust fists. At the center of it all, suffused with five hundred years of barbaric and bloody history, still sits the ancient Kremlin like a giant spider within its web—dangerous, forbidding and inscrutable.

To the visitor who was last in Moscow in 1936, the year Stalin's paranoia burst out in the first of the great "treason trials," Moscow seems surprisingly the same today. Of course, the skyscrapers are new; the enormous housing projects that have extended the city limits far outward in every direction are new; the overcrowded trolleys have disappeared in favor of less overcrowded buses; auto traffic has vastly increased; clothes are somewhat better and shortages of consumer goods visibly less acute—but Moscow is still the same frenetic, mysterious, rigid and unfriendly giant it has ever been.

Since Stalin's death, things have obviously eased up; and the foreign visitor returning to look around Russia after only five years' absence is apt to note far more change in atmosphere than the one returning after a quarter-century. This apparent paradox is easily explained: in the interval, a devastating war had occurred with the inevitable drop in standards of living from the already low level of the thirties. On top of that, especially toward the end of his reign, Stalin's ultra-reactionary policies reached new lows even for the history of imperial Russia. Badly off as the Soviet Union was in the thirties, it was much worse off in the forties and early fifties. Therefore the present stage of Soviet development shows—in life, liberty and the pursuit of happiness—an improvement more striking when compared with only a few years ago than with the earlier period.

This is not a question of material welfare only, but rather of the intangibles that give the tone of political and intellectual life that any Westerner naturally looks for when he visits a Communist country. In the mid-thirties, the Soviet Union was a despotic dictatorship whose statist philosophy was alien to Western ideas of individual rights and human dignity, just as it is today. Yet in that period, it was easier for an ordinary traveler in Soviet Russia to find a basis for intellectual contact with the Russian man in the street, to converse with him on mutually understood premises, than it is today.

In light of the much touted "liberalizing" of the post-Stalin era, how can this be possible? The reason is simply that in the 1930's the bulk of adult, educated Russians, then in their middle years, had grown up in a Western-oriented social environment, in which they had naturally become familiar with Western cultural values. No matter how anti-capitalist and anti-Western they might have learned to be in the revolutionary period, these Russians had spent their formative years with at least some contact with Western thought, language and literature. The West, in brief, was not totally foreign to them; and even the fanatically doctrinaire Communists among them had, by and large, an understanding of the Western viewpoint.

In the thirties, these were the people with whom one would have contact in Russia—people then aged from twenty-five to sixty. Now, twenty-five to thirty years later, these are the older generation; and the new have grown up completely within the confines of Communist ideology and Communist schooling, touched by an absolute minimum of contact with and knowledge of the West.

The Russian Revolution took place well over forty years ago; virtually all Russians less than sixty have had adult experience of only a Communist-enclosed society. Except for a few specialists and scientists, they know nothing of the West, have been afforded no opportunity even to understand the premises of Western culture, and therefore can hardly establish any real philosophic contact with Westerners. This is why, with the exceptions noted, when an ordinary Russian and an ordinary American meet today and try to engage in an ordinary conversation on general political or cultural— as distinct from specific scientific or technical—subjects, a failure in communication is likely to result. Thus, it still is harder to establish a common premise to serve as a basis of intelligible discussion between a non-specialist Russian and American today than it was twenty-five years ago. And despite the widely publicized Russian emphasis on the study of languages, it seemed easier in 1936 to find a Russian in the streets or shops or hotels or offices of Moscow or Leningrad or Kiev who spoke English, French or German than it does today.

This situation is, of course, not static. The new emphasis on language instruction, the cautious lowering of barriers against travel abroad, the great increase in foreign visitors to the U.S.S.R., the hesitant encouragement of exchange of persons (limited thus far, however, largely to technical specialists), and, above all, the rising standard of living in Russia that brings with it a growing demand for contact with the outside world—all these factors tend to open paths to intercommunication, and with it increased knowledge and perhaps even increased understanding.

There is an invisible wall—a kind of plastic curtain—that the ordinary visitor from the West is likely to come up against as he tries to get to know Russia and the Russians. He can see them, he can talk to them, but he will find it exceedingly difficult to get *through* to them. And still he will be greeted everywhere he goes with innumerable expressions of friendliness on the part of the individual Soviet citizen, whom the constant stream of violent anti-Western propaganda does not seem to have affected on a personal plane at all, either in Moscow or—even less so—in Russia's provincial cities.

The abysmal ignorance of the average Russian about the West in general and the United States in particular is matched only by the amiability of the average Russian toward the American visitor. In Moscow's famous subway (decorated with such items as a portrait bust of Stalin in gold mosaic) a young man rises to give his seat to an American woman, addressing her in English. When asked how he happens to know the language he replies with a grin, "By listening to the BBC." . . . A man sitting next to an American at one of Moscow's thirty or forty legitimate theaters courteously inquires if he can help explain the meaning of that evening's performance, and takes great pains in doing so. . . . On a bench in Rostov's city park, the two soldiers who speak only Russian spend an earnest hour trying to make the American who speaks no Russian understand—via sign language, pictures and a very few words of German that they picked up during the war. Understand what? Nothing of any importance—just the simplest human data as to families, business, education, travel. These two young Russians radiantly enjoyed even the most rudimentary contact with a Westerner—in the shadow of a billboard full of viciously anti-American posters.

Knowing that it would take hours or, more probably, days to arrange officially a visit to a dormitory at Stalingrad's Medical Institute in order to see how the students actually live, the two foreigners decide to do it unofficially. Luck is with them; the "house mother" of the coed dormitory welcomes them cordially as soon as she understands the reason for their visit. She leads the two strangers to a room chosen at random, the neat bedroom of four young women students. By sustained effort on both sides, it is possible to communicate.

Word spreads rapidly about the dormitory that foreigners are there. Students gather at the open doorway, shyly at first, then pushed forward into the room by others—laughing uproariously but sympathetically with the Americans striving to cross the language barrier. The crowd continually grows larger, prompted by the typical and unmistakable mixture of friendliness and curiosity that characterizes the attitude of the ordinary Russian citizen toward Americans.

The crush soon becomes so great that the visitors have to separate and move to larger rooms, each finding himself surrounded by at least fifty young men and women ranging in age from twenty to thirty. Not one of these medical students speaks any Western European language, except for a few words of halting German, a hangover from the war.

Do students get paid salaries in America? How long does medical training take there? Can Negroes go to school? Are there jobs for all after graduation? Why do your generals want war?

When the visitors patiently explain that nobody in America,

generals included, wants war, the students burst into applause. And when after an hour and a half of friendly if laborious interchange it is time to go, a mass of students troop through the corridors and down the stairs behind their visitors, like children following twin Pied Pipers. At the front door, the students break spontaneously into applause, and shouts of "good-by"—the only English heard all evening—and "*auf wiedersehen*" speed the guests on their way—as against every lighted window of the dormitory's front there stand silhouetted two or three figures of students, men and women, leaning out to wave farewell.

Although it does not approach the liberalization in Yugoslavia, or even, with all its retrogression, in Poland, the "liberalization" that has taken place in the Soviet Union since the death of Stalin is evident in many ways: a more relaxed attitude toward foreigners; an end to secret arrests and shooting without trial; a partial decentralization of economic controls; more freedom for the arts; more attention to consumer goods; a new emphasis on exchange of visitors with the Free World. But all of this is relative.

No foreign papers, except Communist ones, are normally available on the newsstands of the U.S.S.R. Such few non-technical foreign books as one can find are usually novels of social significance— though Shakespeare, as well as other Western classical writers, is familiar on the Russian stage. In the great Lenin Library in Moscow, claimed to be the biggest in the world, a fairly large selection of foreign periodicals is available, but not on the open shelves. They —and many foreign books—can be obtained only by special permission. A librarian who is asked about the restricted shelves is rather reluctant to discuss the matter but "thinks" that the works of Koestler, Kafka, Silone, Trotsky—to mention a few at random— would be so treated. "After all," she adds, "I know that you have exactly the same system in the libraries of the United States"— and neither denial nor argument can convince her to the contrary.

"Why should we permit Western newspapers to be sold here? Why should we allow your broadcasts to be heard?" demands one of the highest Soviet officials dealing with cultural affairs. "Why should we subject our people to the insults of foreigners? If there are hooligans in the street and they stone your house, you board up the windows to protect yourself, don't you—and that's what we're doing here." And the answer (by none other than Deputy Premier Frol Kozlov) to a complaint about the anti-American posters in every public park: "Well, that only shows that we have freedom of the press."

In farms as well as factory, workers are egged on unceasingly not only by the material incentive of more pay for more product but also by the moral pressure of a ubiquitous propaganda machine drilling into them the patriotic necessity of constantly increasing their production. This was called Stakhanovism in the 1930's. Today it is so normal it has no special name, but along with it goes a genuine pride in product as well as productivity.

Whatever the human and social costs of increasing production, the fundamental fact about the Soviet Union today is that it is producing more; there are more goods for peace and war available all the time; the standard of living is rising; investment abroad, in satellites and underdeveloped countries, is increasing; a new class of managers is rapidly developing, with what social results no one yet can accurately predict.

The "self-made man" whose advancement is due more to technical and administrative proficiency than to political orthodoxy is appearing in Soviet industrial society. One of this new class, deputy director of Moscow's great tractor and bicycle plant (forty thousand employees), takes especial pride in the sobriquet, and also in needling American visitors with the information that after a visit to the United States a few years ago, when he was unable to purchase a particular kind of stamping machine (which might have been turned to military production), he came back home and made one of his own that is now used throughout the Soviet Union.

Through the exceedingly efficient but rigid educational system, recently revised to favor vocational training, literacy—but not knowledge—is becoming universal. Even Russia's traditional alcoholism is claimed to be decreasing, but some observers believe this boast is unfounded. In any event, the war against it and against many less serious human failings is carried on with puritanical relish by the Communist youth organizations, which sanctimoniously busy themselves with improving public morals.

It can be argued that the self-confidence, the xenophobia mixed with an intense popular desire for peace, the concentration of the people (if not their leaders) on their own internal affairs, the smug conviction that theirs is the only good society, the refusal to acknowledge any debt (intellectual or otherwise) to the outside world, the faith that their virgin territories in Siberia are the hope of the future—all of this, one may argue, is only symptomatic of any pioneer society in its shakedown stage. But no pioneer society has ever before had a hydrogen bomb in the hands of its rulers.

CHAPTER 13

Hate, Fear and Hope: Poland

The distance from Moscow to Warsaw is more than the several hundred miles on the map or the few hours it takes the small Soviet plane (flying characteristically below one thousand feet) to make the trip. It is the distance between a smug, self-satisfied capital whose every brick and turret speaks of imperial Russia's eternal characteristics, suspicion and power; and a restive, shabby and exciting city that for all its Communist overlay is reaching out for contact with the Western world.

As if to drive home the fact that the Soviet Union towers over Poland, the building that dominates all Warsaw is the Soviet Union's gift to the Polish people—the "Palace of Culture" with Stalin's name engraved above the door, as arrogant a present as one government could possibly devise for another. This monstrous structure glowers down upon the city, throwing its shadow across smashed and miserable habitations and across the skeletal office building that was headquarters of the Warsaw uprising during the war—the uprising savagely repressed by the Germans while the Russian armies sat silently a cannon-shot distant across the Vistula. Warsaw is a city from which the war seems only as far away as yesterday, with its acres of rubble, its dozens of bomb-scarred and half-wrecked buildings, its shoddy new apartment houses long since occupied, though their walls are still unfinished and pipes and wiring still exposed.

To those who knew Warsaw before the war, it is all but unrecognizable now. But standing out in a sea of ruins among scattered islands of new construction, are the ancient houses and churches of "Stare Miasto," the Old Town, on a bluff above the Vistula. They appear miraculously new and untouched amid the fifteen-year-old wreckage of the war. On closer inspection it turns out that they actually are new and untouched. They represent a typically romantic and typically Polish expression of defiance against the Nazis' effort to uproot the physical traces of Polish culture by systematically destroying all that was old and historic in the nation's capital. In a city where the postwar housing shortage is probably more acute than in any other metropolis of Europe, the utilitarian materialists who govern Poland decided to give first priority in their limited resources to reconstructing the old town precisely in its ancient style, including even such details as reproductions of lamps, clocks, murals, inscriptions—all like a Hollywood stage set masking the reality of wartime ruins that still surround the medieval ramparts of old Warsaw.

When you walk about the ruins of Poland's capital, which was 85 per cent destroyed by the Nazis—and still today looks raw and dismal—you understand a little better the preoccupation of the Poles with Germany. Even if Poland were totally independent of the Soviet Union, it is difficult to believe that Polish foreign policy would be very different from what it is. The outlook of Poland, and of practically all Poles, is conditioned by the passionate desire to see the Oder-Neisse border internationally recognized and ratified, by the conviction that German reunification would be dangerous for them, and by the belief that a *détente* in central Europe would make life more bearable for Poland, caught as it is in the age-old squeeze between its neighbors.

Even in the one vibrant center of opposition to Communist ideology and extremism—the Polish Catholic Church—there is no dissent on the German question. If you visit one of Poland's leading Catholic politicians, a confidant of the Cardinal himself, he will tell you that all Poles see exactly alike on Germany: "We will retain the western provinces; we will never feel secure until the Germans recognize the border; we fear German rearmament more than any other development in Europe. The Germans will eventually come to dominate NATO, especially if the restraining hand of America is removed." This thought leads inescapably to the paradoxical conclusion widely (but privately) held by many Poles that it is to their interest not that the "Yankees go home," as the Russians desire, but rather that the United States remain in strength and influence on the European Continent.

The Poles may hate the Russians, but they fear and hate the Germans. The Russians have already taken all the Polish territory they want; and so, in a sense, they have done their worst. They stand now as military protectors of Poland's western frontier, which in Polish eyes is menaced by Germany despite Chancellor Adenauer's repeated assertions that he will never seek a readjustment of the Polish border by force. American diplomatic support for the re-armament of West Germany would alone be enough to range the Poles against the United States in the international arena, even if the Communist question did not exist. It is true that East Germany has also been armed, and with Russian help; but the Poles see no possibility of an attack from that quarter so long as it remains under Soviet control. The unremitting fear of Germany is a reality not only in Poland but through much of Europe, and is neither limited to areas of Soviet control nor caused (though it is used) by Soviet propaganda.

There are forces, in Germany as well as in Poland, working toward a relaxation of that fear. An indication that they may be making headway was afforded by the recent visits to Poland, with Adenauer's unspoken blessing, of Berthold Beitz, the dynamic young general manager of the Krupp industrial empire, who has long held the unorthodox position in the Ruhr that the West Germans can and must establish sounder relations with the Polish "People's Republic."

Sharing a common frontier with the Soviet Union and forced to accept a common ideology, Poland still is struggling with remarkable success to preserve its own individuality both nationally and ideologically. The crisis of October '56 was a turning point in the life of Poland as a satellite state, when the threat of armed revolt forced the Soviet Union to relax its rule. Gomulka, Poland's owl-like leader, is no Tito; but as a loyal Communist he was able to extract some concessions from Moscow. Ever since, he has been engaged in the difficult feat of walking the tightrope between Polish nationalism and Russian Communism without doing too much violence to either. Since '56, the police terror has all but disappeared; since '56 the relations with the Church have turned from open warfare to an armed truce; collectivization of the agricultural peasantry has been halted; the economic organization of Polish industry has been to some extent decentralized—less than in Yugoslavia, but more than in the U.S.S.R. Most important of all, the atmosphere of repression, of utter degradation of the individual spirit that was an inescapable mark of Stalinism, has been partially lifted.

While Poland surely is not free, it is incomparably freer than it was, even though since early in 1959 there has been a considerable retightening of the screws. Nowhere else behind the Iron Curtain could one see a performance of Kafka's *The Trial* played before a packed (and well-dressed) audience. In no other satellite would such a Western-oriented popular weekly as *Przekroj* (*Cross-Section*) be tolerated, whose Western outlook is revealed in matters of style and taste. But on matters political, in the words of one of this magazine's editors, "We go to the movies." In no other Communist country except perhaps Yugoslavia could there be such heated—and informed—arguments over modern art and philosophy; nor in any other has such striking *avant-garde* talent made its appearance in painting and in sculpture.

If the city's aspect is grim, the same cannot be said for the people who throng its streets, who on Sunday crowd into its churches, who jostle each other in its stores, who fill its restaurants and its theaters and its night spots. There is a vitality in the Warsaw atmosphere that is almost visible; and the visitor will experience the same sense of electricity in other cities too—Cracow in the south, for instance, or Wroclaw to the west.

In Wroclaw, principal city of the former German provinces, a dynamic young governor still in his thirties is operating with a surprising degree of local autonomy in such areas as industrial production, in management of state-owned enterprises (which means practically all of them) and in distribution of profits. "We've used the profits of one factory to buy a TV station from Germany, for which the central government in Warsaw put up no money at all," he tells his visitors with evident pride. "Our next project is to purchase an artificial heart and lungs from the United States to modernize research in our medical institute," which, when the city was known as Breslau, was famed throughout the world.

The western provinces have been so thoroughly Polonized that it is now difficult to find any Germans in them at all. Wroclaw before the war had a population of 600,000, almost entirely German. Today it has 400,000, of whom a few hundred are German. Many of the new Polish inhabitants came from those parts of eastern Poland seized by the Soviet Union—a theft of territory that Communist Poles now prefer to forget. Wroclaw itself was almost as completely destroyed during the war as Warsaw, and it is even less rebuilt. Acres of rubble, patched-up buildings, broken walls are seen on every hand; yet the Mayor will roll off long lists of figures to show how reconstruction is moving ahead. "In the first ten years, Warsaw got all the materials," he says, "but now we're getting some, and soon you won't recognize this city." One can only hope he is right, given the picture of devastation Wroclaw represents today.

The two professors were discussing at the dinner table how much freedom they have. "There's no pressure at all on us to join the Communist party. Most of us are not members because the membership means too much extra work, and no extra pay. As it is, we professors are economically worse off than before the war."

"What about freedom?"

"Well, in economics and political science, our freedom is limited —we have to teach the Marxist point of view—but we also can, and many of us do, give other interpretations as well. Remember that many prewar Polish professors are now back at their old stands. We certainly aren't held to an exclusive presentation of Marxism—"

"In what we teach," interrupted the other, "but in what we write, I'd say we're more limited. Anyway," he added, with the trace of a smile, "I guess—considering what it might have been—we have enough academic freedom for one man's lifetime."

For a few years after 1956, the study of Marxism was not even required in Polish universities. But that era of liberalism has come to an end; and now compulsory lectures on various aspects of Communist doctrine have been restored to the curriculum.

The young writer who ekes out a living by translating foreign books and journals was muttering in a crowded bar. "Four years ago I couldn't even have been seen talking to a foreigner—that's an indication of how things have improved. I still find it difficult to earn a living because my distaste for Communism is well known. But I do manage to live, and to get hold of Western books—and I am not afraid to talk." He looked around the room suspiciously and said suddenly, "We've been together here too long—let's adjourn to my apartment." He continued talking there, but turned up the radio in order to neutralize any listening device the police might have concealed within the walls.

"You know, I'm a moral man; but in order to live in this country, you have to steal. Everybody has to steal, or to buy things from someone else who has stolen them. If you want to paint your room, you can hire a private painter, but where will he have found the paint? Stolen it from the government, of course. If you want anything repaired, where will you get the materials? They're stolen from the government, of course. The effect of this universal thievery on public morality is going to be serious after a time; but it's inevitable in an economy so short of consumers' goods and so rigidly managed as a Communist state must be."

Poles cannot easily find non-Communist publications from the West on their newsstands, but they can subscribe to them. Their chances of receiving such material varies with the political temperature. One French review distinguished for its liberal anti-Communist outlook has built up "since October" (1956) a subscription list of several hundreds in Poland. However, with the contraction of liberties that came about in 1959, about half the copies of each issue were confiscated by the Polish censor. Somehow, quite a few of them found their way to secondhand bookstores via the black market. Result: anybody who hadn't received his own copy of the magazine could buy it clandestinely at only a modestly inflated price.

Pointing to a picture of the Virgin Mary in his sparsely furnished room, the well-known Catholic member of Parliament traced with his finger the three words of the inscription surmounting her figure: "Maria Regina Poloniae." He paused a moment. "That's the phrase —'Queen of Poland'—that bites most deeply into the Communist façade. Those are the words that combine a deep religious faith with an even deeper nationalism. There you have the key to Poland's resistance to untrammeled control by a Communist, Russian-dominated political machine."

He was now speaking intensely, but quietly, and without bitterness. "We have to take the existence of the Polish Communist state as a fact," he was saying. "Our problem is not to overthrow it— which would be impossible now or any other time with Russia as our neighbor. Our problem is to live with it, to create conditions under which our church can continue to exist. This isn't a question of ideology; it's a question of survival in the only Communist country where the Church can still survive, and where Catholics like myself can be elected to Parliament.

"It isn't even a question of getting rid of Soviet influence. Poland's economy is now dependent on Russia's—we couldn't live now without her—and in any case it's Russia alone that protects our western frontier. No, our problem is less with the U.S.S.R. than it is with the government of Poland. It's odd, though, that the more pressure the state puts on, the more support we get from the people, and the more strongly we dig in our heels. It's when the pressures ease that we feel the weakening hold of religion especially among the youth, and the growth of laicism especially among people uprooted from their former homes. The situation of the Church has again been worsening recently—but it's still better than 'before October,' when I wouldn't have dared to talk to foreigners at all.''

Next door to the present Polish Foreign Office were the German secret police headquarters, where the cells and torture instruments are still preserved, and where defiant messages scribbled by doomed prisoners on the walls can still be read. The Poles have neither forgotten nor forgiven.

In his well-appointed office, the Polish diplomat puffed thoughtfully on his pipe as he said to his American visitor: "Whether we like it or not, and whether you like it or not, we can never in the visible future return to our old relations with the West—because of Germany, because of our geography, and because of our own economic and political system. But we can be useful to the West. Within the Soviet bloc, we can exercise some influence. We can't serve as a bridge because none of the big powers wants a bridge; but we can be a persuasive element inside our own bloc.

"Poland's greatest interest lies in a *détente*. We're like a turtle: when there's relaxation of tensions, we can stick our own necks out a bit, but when things tighten up, we have to retreat into the shell of our own security. We don't overestimate our possibilities; but we think we know more about the Western mind than the Russians do, and can understand it better. Therefore we have a role to play with our allies of the East—if the West only gives us a chance to prove it."

If the West only gives the Poles a chance to prove it—but how? The Polish vote in the U.N. is consistently a Soviet-bloc vote. The Poles in foreign policy show little deviation from the Russian line. Poland is economically chained to the Soviet Union. Poland is no neutralist. For all its inner ferment, Poland is a satellite; but Poland nevertheless offers to the United States the greatest possibility of maintaining effective entree to the Soviet-dominated world.

While very few innovations in the arena of international politics can be expected from the lesser Communist states, it is only common sense to lend attention on the rare occasions when such proposals are made. The Rapacki Plan, put forward by Poland for denuclearization of a central European zone, was unacceptable to the West; but, in the obviously desirable effort to encourage independent thinking among the satellites, this suggestion of the Polish Foreign Minister ought to have been given something more than the brusque, almost automatic, rejection it received.

Poland is not going to be pulled out of the Soviet bloc but the Polish mentality still looks westward; Poland has an identity and a personality of its own; and the stream of Polish good will toward America and the Americans still runs broad and deep. This is why the exchange programs with Poland, conducted principally by the Ford Foundation, under which scores of Polish intellectuals have been enabled to breathe Western air for several weeks or even months, are so important. It is why the fullest flow of trade and traffic between Poland and the United States is worth encouraging. It is why the indication of a friendlier relationship after the Herter-Gomulka talks in the fall of 1960 is so hopeful, reinforced by a special gesture to Poland in President Kennedy's first State of the Union message. It is why continuation of American aid to Poland is so vital and amendment of the restrictive Battle Act so necessary.

Since 1956, direct American aid has amounted to over $500 million, most of which was in agricultural surplus. This aid has tended to fluctuate with the political climate. In 1959, when the Poles were taking a particularly strong line in support of the U.S.S.R., a projected American assistance program was curtailed; in 1960, when the Poles agreed to compensate American citizens for property seizures, our aid went up again.

This is a time-honored but delicate game to play; and it can only be played successfully within the limits of Polish potentialities for independent action. It would be unrealistic for us to expect a true *quid pro quo* for our assistance at the present time. It would be foolish to think that we can persuade or bribe the Poles to vote or move against the Russians. The most and the least we can do is to continue to demonstrate to Poland that we of the West have not ostracized her, that we are willing to keep the door open to whatever response the Poles may be able to make.

Poland has retrogressed since 1956 in political and economic freedom, on the farms, in the factories, in the towns. But Poland still is the least doctrinaire and therefore should be to us the most hopeful element of the Soviet satellite system.

CHAPTER 14

Between Two Worlds: Yugoslavia

Warsaw has for generations been a city of intellectual distinction, while even as the capital of a sovereign kingdom, Belgrade's tradition has been just the opposite. Despite Russian omnipresence in Warsaw, the ferment of thought, of speech, of artistic endeavor, of intellectual life is far more marked in Poland's capital than in Yugoslavia's. The Poles had a richer base from which to start than the Yugoslavs, and the results are richer—though the Poles are handicapped because they do not have the independence that the Yugoslavs won for themselves.

"Don't ever forget that Yugoslavia is basically Communist," said the Western diplomat as he strolled through the garden of his home on the heights above Belgrade. "Too many of my colleagues are beguiled by the apparent liberalism of this regime and by its quarrel with the Soviet Union. But Tito can go only just so far in our direction; he and all the people around him are devoted Communists, and it's a major mistake to forget it."

Mindful of that warning, the observer looks about Belgrade, a metropolis of 600,000 people almost devoid of motor traffic (there are only 6,000 private cars in the entire country), booming with building activity but, with few exceptions, architecturally undistinguished. One of the exceptions is the new capitol, a huge and handsome modern structure placed—like the Pentagon in Washington, of which it is slightly reminiscent—on low land across the Sava River facing the city proper. Years in the making, the clean modernity of "New Belgrade" contrasts sharply with the heavy turn-of-the-century Austrian-style government buildings in the rest of the city. Despite all the recent construction, Belgrade has a dowdy appearance, heightened by the pockmarked houses and scraggly parks that testify to the latest of the many bombardments it has suffered during the centuries as the price of its strategic location at a principal gateway between the Christian and the Moslem worlds.

There is in Belgrade very little of the antique left. There is also, happily, very little of the Russian modern. The break between Tito and Stalin in 1948 came just in time to save Yugoslavia's capital from the worst of the Stalinesque architectural atrocities that have been visited on Warsaw and on Moscow. One new "skyscraper" block was originally planned as a Communist Youth center; but at the time of the rupture, the Yugoslavs decided they needed a new hotel more than another party building. So, with the aid of American counterpart funds, it was turned into a pseudo-Hiltonesque hostelry where the lights go out at unexpected moments but the plumbing usually works. In the morning its lobbies are filled with businessmen and tourists speaking every language of Europe; after dark it is jammed with bourgeois-looking Serbo-Croats, dancing and night-clubbing after the rigors of a working day that normally begins at seven A.M. and ends at two or three in the afternoon.

The visitor returning to Yugoslavia for the first time in twenty-five years finds one thing that has not changed in intensity, but even this has changed in direction. It is the spirit of nationalism. Before the war the emphasis was on the nationalisms of the various groups that make up Yugoslavia: the Serbs, Croats, Slovenes, Macedonians, Montenegrins and others who, when not fighting against outside invaders, have been spending the centuries in religious and political warfare against each other. During the Second World War they succeeded in doing both things at the same time. What came out of that dreadful period of the early forties, at frightful cost, was a more unified country than went in. This wartime experience is the key to Yugoslavia today. Under Tito's stimulus the nationalism of the Yugoslavs has tended to coalesce into a Yugoslavian nationalism.

"You must remember that the Communist leaders of our country, unlike the rulers of the Russian satellites, do have genuine roots in the people as national heroes," observed an old bourgeois politician who has managed to survive through all the changes. "It was the Communist partisans who formed a principal nucleus of resistance against the Nazi invader. Tito is a revered national hero as well as a Communist chieftain; and his party and his leadership have a special hold in Yugoslavia quite apart from political or economic ideology. The fundamental difference between us and the other Socialist [Communist] states of Eastern Europe is that they were 'liberated' by the Russians—we did it for ourselves." Still divided by bitter memories and linguistic and religious differences, the Yugoslavs are nevertheless today far more closely united as a nation than they ever were before the war and revolution.

Defiance of Russian control and determination to develop its own form of Communism combine to give to Belgrade a peculiar quality unlike that of any other Communist capital. Western newspapers are sold freely on the streets, Western plays are given in the theater, Western visitors are cordially welcomed by officials, by factory workers, by party functionaries, by professional people—artists, writers, actors, researchers—by anyone who has anything to say. And they say it with relative freedom—not our kind of freedom, but with more freedom than one would expect in a Communist society.

The noted editor, a loyal member of the party, is explaining the difference between Yugoslav and Russian Communism as he sips the inevitable cup of thick, strong coffee that is a legacy from Ottoman days and is served every time two men sit down for more than a three-minute chat.

"We insist on national independence and on the possibility of socialism thriving in different countries in different ways. We think that our country can and will, in fact, develop its own kind of socialism suitable to its own needs. We don't believe it should be forced from outside to conform to a preconceived idea, or to one particular interpretation of Marx or Lenin. If you ask me, that's the biggest difference between us and the Russians: independence for ourselves and a belief that socialism can take many and varied forms. For instance, your country already has important socialistic aspects to it, as any industrialized Western country has. Socialism is being and will be achieved in the West without either war or revolution.

"It's for these two reasons—independence of action for ourselves and diversity for socialism everywhere—that we're ostracized by the Russians, who see in our philosophy a threat to their own pretensions. We'd like to be friends with Russia, of course—but we'll never join the Soviet or any other bloc. Naturally we know that the Soviets are a greater danger to us than the United States could ever be; but don't imagine we like all aspects of American foreign policy either. We appreciate American aid, which was given to us when we really needed help; but you're too tied up with reactionary governments throughout the globe. Furthermore, we—like most Europeans—think Germany divided is safer for the rest of us than Germany united. No blocs for us; this is a windy part of the world, and the wind blows cold from the east."

Every Yugoslav emphasizes with pride the internal differences between Soviet Communism and Tito's Communism. They all—from trained economists familiar with the West to factory managers hardly out of their twenties—start off by using the word "decentralization." Although the Yugoslavs claim to have a relatively free market, with two-thirds of their prices based on supply and demand, there is more and tighter control than meets the eye. Yet while foreign trade has until recently been manipulated through variable exchange rates, and an *ad hoc* taxation system has helped manage the internal economy, the tendency is clearly toward liberalization. Under new fiscal and foreign exchange reforms effected with the support of large Western credits, Yugoslavia is moving rapidly away from orthodox Communist trading practices. The West already accounts for 75 per cent of Yugoslavia's foreign trade; establishment of the new policies will permit Yugoslavia to enjoy a degree of currency convertibility unknown to the rest of the Communist world and will move Marshal Tito's domain economically ever closer to the West.

The projected new constitution of 1962 will make firmer a progressive decentralization in party as well as in economic affairs. The various industries and enterprises of Yugoslavia partially govern themselves even now by autonomous "workers' councils" which are elected within each plant and, generally speaking, decide on wages, prices and production schedules and distribution of profits. "We start from the interest of the individual, the Soviets from the interest of the state"—that is the fundamental distinction in which most Yugoslavs believe. And, despite the rising cost of living, they have a clearly rising standard of living to fortify their conviction that the system works for Yugoslavia.

"We haven't political democracy in the sense of competitive political parties," says a young official, "but don't get the idea that the citizen has no voice in his own affairs. In the factory, office or even theater, there are the workers' councils that run the place, all duly elected. Then there are all sorts of elective citizens' organizations that manage schools, hospitals, housing and all the social organisms, below the elected local councils and state and national parliaments."

There is even private enterprise, especially among artisans. An individual may employ up to a half-dozen workers; but the bulk of commerce and industry is carried out by co-operative organizations. The latter extend to the manufacture of even such passing fads as hula hoops. During the craze in 1958-59, an imaginative private entrepreneur began selling hoops in Belgrade at the profitable price of two dollars a hoop, until one of the co-ops seized the idea and put him out of business by marketing them at half that.

Under their unorthodox form of Communism, the Yugoslavs have been encouraging foreign commercial interest in their country through un-Communist-sounding licensing agreements. Actually, over eight hundred Yugoslav enterprises now hold licensing rights from European manufacturers; and the Yugoslavs are seeking to acquire still more in the United States. Foreign corporations are not allowed any control over operations of a Yugoslav factory; but they naturally profit from the sale of manufacturing rights as well as of specific equipment. As one Yugoslav official says: "A foreign corporation may not get an equity here but its money is safe. In Latin America, for instance, it may acquire an equity but is always liable to nationalization. We've had our nationalization."

A police state? Yes, by democratic standards; but no, compared to its eastern neighbors. There is little direct censorship of the press —though recently one edition of a humorous weekly featuring an anti-Russian cartoon was seized, but seized a day or two after it appeared on the newsstands, which was a long enough interval for anyone to buy it who wanted to. There is no direct control of the arts—no nonsense any more about "socialist realism"—but in no medium would an artist think of attacking the government. The Yugoslav stage presents everything from Shakespeare to O'Neill; painting is enjoying a boom encouraged both directly and indirectly by the state. In every government office one sees the work of Yugoslav artists, just as one used to see WPA paintings in every office in Washington. The topmost artists live relatively well— which isn't too difficult for anyone whose salary reaches the heights of $2,000 or $2,500 a year. A prima donna of the Belgrade stage is such a "millionaire." For a relatively good apartment of three or four rooms in the heart of Belgrade, she pays ten or twelve dollars a month.

Freedom of speech exists within limits. "We tolerate a good deal of talk, but of course no anti-government action," says a Communist official with a grim smile. One is struck by the number of youngish men as well as women attending services in the Orthodox cathedral; but the Church has lost all its former political power. Freedom of travel exists within limits, too, as is proved by the large number of Yugoslavs who somehow find the means to visit neighboring Italy. So many of them, in fact, that in one recent year the government put a temporary ban on such travel, not for political reasons but to preserve needed foreign exchange. Even former bourgeois who left the country after the revolution are allowed freely to return as long as they are not considered war criminals or enemies of the state.

Nowadays when a man falls out of favor with the regime he is no longer summarily shot but may be deprived of the right to work, the right to travel, virtually of the right to live—with all the ingenuity and remorselessness of the true police state. There are not many such people nowadays; but there are a few, and the existence of even one of them is sufficient reminder that Yugoslavia is still a long way from liberal democracy. Vladimir Dedijer, intimate friend and biographer of Tito, was one such victim; but after nearly starving (he had turned over to the Communist party large royalties for a hospital that was never built) he was at last allowed to go abroad to earn a living through non-political lectures. Milovan Djilas, former Vice-President of Yugoslavia, was another, and the most famous. Author of *The New Class*, which bitterly attacked Tito's policies, he had been sentenced to several years in prison; but in 1961, after having served less than half his term, he was suddenly released in what was widely interpreted as a gesture by Tito to Western European liberals.

The dissenters who are really hated and to a degree feared are the unregenerate Stalinists who have never in their hearts followed Tito in his break with the Soviet Union more than a decade ago. While he talks of coexistence and independent socialist development, they think of the inevitability of violent class struggle and of war.

"You have your revolutionists," said one of the highest officials of the Yugoslav government to the American visitor, "and we have our counter-revolutionists. Your Communist party is small and of no importance while your country is great and powerful. Therefore you can afford a broad degree of political liberalism. Our country is small and in constant danger from the East, so we have to combat the enemies of our state with methods that we don't particularly like, and I hope won't always have to use. A police state, you say? Well, I don't approve your choice of words; let's just say we sometimes have to fight counter-revolution by non-democratic means."

Although political refugees are still escaping every day across the border to Austria and Italy, there is little detectable opposition to the regime, especially to Tito; and the consensus is that at least as long as he lives Yugoslavia will continue to preserve its present course of precarious balance between two worlds.

After Tito—who knows? It is as difficult to think of Yugoslavia without Tito as it is to think of France without de Gaulle. His successor may be the schoolmasterish First Vice-President Edvard Kardelj or the tough Minister of the Interior Aleksandar Rankovic, or both—the former becoming head of government, the latter party chieftain. They might well be able to continue working together, as they have had long experience in doing. Whatsoever the succession, it will surely follow the same tight path of neo-Communism that Tito has been following under Russia's shadow but out from under Russia's heel.

Part III

CHAPTER 15

The New World
Faces a Newer One

The evolution of the Communist world in Eastern Europe is far from complete; the revolution in Africa has hardly begun. To become effective in these areas, American policy can follow no such stereotypes of political action as it did in Asia after the Second World War, when the new countries were more often judged by sion, it will surely follow the same tight path of neo-Communism the militancy of their anti-Communism alone than by their efforts to fulfill the wants of their people.

In subsaharan Africa now we have a unique opportunity because we are in on the ground floor; we have little record of official contact, good or bad, with most of its underdeveloped countries. We can approach them with a fresh outlook and a flexible one, spurred by the knowledge that in our own continent the Cuban problem might not have developed as it did had we recognized more quickly the needs of the Cuban people. We can afford no more Cubas in Latin America, though we are threatened with many; and we can afford no Cubas in Africa either, where it still may not be too late to head them off. But the time is short.

119

The traditional American attitude, in which all Communist and leftist states are reckoned as of a piece with the Soviet Union, is out of date. It is illustrated by the characteristic American approach to the countries of the uncommitted world, where we have tended to judge them in our own image, their needs by our desires, their internal conflicts by our external policies.

Our attitudes need not only revision; they need re-evaluation. We require a re-education in political tolerance, in the realization that although we have one of the oldest functioning political systems extant, it may not precisely fit all needs of all the newer lands.

In this changing world, we Americans will have to get used to the idea that the problem for us in the new states of Africa (and Asia) is to combat the growth and dynamics of the new Russian Empire in the uncommitted countries rather than the social or economic system that in their rush toward "modernization" they may develop for themselves. We cannot do very much about the particular form of political or economic system chosen by the new states, while there is a good deal we can do about the efforts of the U.S.S.R. or the U.A.R. to include these states within their own spheres of influence.

But all our efforts will be heavily handicapped as long as widespread racial discrimination exists in the United States. As a 1961 report to the Senate stated, this "probably is the most important of all the natural barriers to a better understanding between Africa and this country."

The new African states can succeed—and if given a chance they will—not as satellites of East or West, not necessarily as free-enterprise parliamentary democracies, but as independent entities growing along African lines out of the African soil. American policy toward them is, or ought to be, to help them stand on their own feet, help them sustain their independence, help them to achieve real freedom of choice in determining their own governmental systems. We must not be deterred from this goal because some of these countries are neutralist, many are socialist and most are, at least for the present, semi-authoritarian. None of these characteristics is in accordance with the American way; but in subsaharan Africa we are going to have to live with them.

The "positive neutralism" so popular along the West African coast expresses a hope and desire to stay out of the power struggle between the Free World and the Soviet Union. It is not that the African states that profess it are necessarily sympathetic to Communism—Ghana, for example, is not, while Guinea is. But Communism, of which they know little, appears less immediate or real a danger to most of them than does colonialism, which they have experienced without exception. They therefore think they can take help from Communist countries at face value, not understanding the danger of Soviet control implicit in Soviet technicians, advisers, administrators and credits.

It is obvious to us that Russian colonialism, not Western colonialism, is the immediate danger to Africa today. It is not so obvious to many Africans, who have experienced only friendly interest from the Soviet Union and the satellites, who know that the French, not Russians, are fighting in Algeria; that Sharpeville is a village in South Africa, not in the Soviet Union. Yet most of the leaders of the new Africa no more wish to be linked with the Soviet Union than they wish to be linked to Western policy. No one has expressed this view more clearly than Kwame Nkrumah, who through his ambitious maneuverings in the Congo played Russia's game—yet who without doubt believes he can remain a free agent immune from the toils of Russian imperialism.

"The cardinal principle upon which the peace and security of this continent depends is the firm insistence that Africa is not an extension of Europe or of any other continent," Nkrumah says. "A corollary of this principle is the resolution that Africa is not going to become a cockpit of the cold war, or a marshaling ground for attack on either West or East, nor is it going to be an arena for fighting out the East-West conflict. In this particular sense, we face neither east nor west; we face forward.

"For the last ten years the tone of international politics has been set by the cold war. We understand the fears on both sides

that have led to this tragic polarization, but Africans have no intention of becoming a part of it."

If the first psychological hurdle for us in Africa is neutralism, the second is socialism. Most of the new African countries are welfare states, many are leftist in economic doctrine and some are quasi-Marxist in concept. How can you expect us to be capitalist, their leaders ask, when we have no capital? The Africans know they need capital, and they know it can best be supplied in the necessary amount only by the outside, capitalist world—though they welcome competition from the Communist world as well. But they also know they have deep-seated social needs that they believe can only be answered by a welfare, or socialist state. While their social and economic theories may bear a resemblance to Marxist doctrine, it is much more accurate to look on their evolution as a genuinely African development, in which the socialist, collectivist features spring out of the African tradition of tribal—or even family—responsibility. The Soviet (and Chinese) menace is great wherever the Russians (or Chinese) have succeeded in penetrating, as in Guinea or Mali or even in Ghana; but it must be distinguished from an indigenous African collectivism.

The tendency to authoritarianism is the third great psychological hurdle for Americans when contemplating massive aid to the new states of tropical Africa. It grows out of the tradition of chieftaincy and it is nurtured by the necessity of creating a stable national state where none had existed before. We have to face the fact that not only are the new African states neutralist in politics, not only are they semi-socialist in economy, but also their practice of government does not necessarily bear a close resemblance to our kind of democracy. Their prime concern has been to establish themselves as viable entities over the forces of tribalism and separatism. Basing their political organization on African tradition, they have tended to create a kind of supratribal state in which the single party, as in Guinea, or the dominant one, as in Ghana, is actually superior to the government itself. It was significant—and entirely to be expected—that in the very first weeks of Congo's independence, and while the country was still in chaos, the then Premier Patrice Lumumba should have announced his intention to suppress the institution of chieftaincy.

The neutralism, the socialism, the authoritarianism of the African states do not affect their willingness to accept economic and technical help whenever they can get it, from East or West, though most of the former colonies still lean strongly toward the West. Help they must have if they are to achieve their freedom, as they have already achieved their independence. To meet the revolution of rising expectations in Africa, as elsewhere in the underdeveloped parts of the globe, is a gigantic task, marked by two basic requirements.

The first requirement is sympathy without condescension for a continent striving to span centuries of human development in years if not in months. The second requirement is assistance in administration, in personnel and in money. Through public and private means, through governments and foundations and banks and businesses and individual enterprise, Africa needs help in every form. It needs investment, it needs technical advice, it needs education on the spot and educational exchanges abroad; it needs basic surveys, it needs roads and dams and doctors and administrators. It needs stability of raw material prices. It needs organization within each country—and closer interchange among them.

It needs all these things without political strings of any sort, express or implied. It needs them because it needs help to stand on its own feet, independent of commitments to either East or West. Neither of these requirements, sympathy nor assistance, has been forthcoming from the United States in the quality or the quantity needed to protect American (let alone African) interests. Sympathy can be expressed in various ways; but the most effective and direct way is through political attitudes and actions. Yet we seemed paralyzed in the voting affecting Africa during the important General Assembly session at the U.N. late in 1960 when the United States failed to use its influence in accordance with the basic American ideal of freedom for all peoples.

This is not to say that the United States ought to desert its European allies to follow every African or Asiatic whim. Our alliances with Britain and France are obviously the keystone of American foreign policy, and they ought to be. But historic friendship, intimate cultural, economic and political ties, and binding military alliances with Western Europe do not mean that the United States must slavishly follow the desire of some or all of its allies in every diplomatic area, especially the extremely delicate one that embraces our relations with the underdeveloped world of the Southern hemisphere.

If we had voted in favor of the anti-colonialism resolution, we would not have broken up NATO nor lost the friendship of the British people. The Canadians voted for it, and so did the Dutch and Italians and Scandinavians and Formosa Chinese. If we had voted in favor of a compromise Algerian resolution, for which Canada and the Scandinavians and the Philippines and Turkey and Uruguay all voted, France would not have liked it; but there are many things the French do, and have a right to do, that we do not like. The existence of an alliance does not imply abrogation of a national responsibility to decide each issue on its merits and in terms of the national interest.

Sympathy as expressed through political means is important; but it is not enough. The other basic requirement is assistance; and in this area too the American effort has been seriously deficient, even though it is also true to say that no nation has been as generous of its aid to others as has our own.

The temptation in Congress is naturally to favor bilateral arrangements in order to get maximum credit for the United States, instead of dissipating it through the international façade of the U.N. But the reasoning is false. As contributor of one-third of the United Nations budget—and in the case of some of the specialized programs even more than that—the United States is known as the principal donor to every country receiving U.N. aid; yet the very fact that it is U.N. aid (and not U.S. aid) makes it usually easier for self-conscious new nations to accept, and makes them less suspicious of the donor's motives.

Except for some of the French colonies that fear Soviet penetration through the U.N., most of the newer countries prefer to receive help via the United Nations as entailing much less risk or danger of political obligation than is implied in bilateral assistance. It was at the very height of the Congo crisis in the summer of 1960 that Dr. Banda of Nyasaland advised the Congolese: "Do not be swayed by either bloc, not by the Eastern bloc nor by the Western bloc. Anything done . . . must be done through the United Nations, and the United Nations only."

The United States can be most effective politically in Africa by not being political at all, by extending the maximum of help through the U.N. to minimize any suggestion that we desire to involve the African states in the struggle between East and West. The United Nations for these reasons must be supported by the United States not merely in words but in new and expanded programs and in cold cash of a magnitude that we have not yet approached.

The U.N. should become the principal instrument of our aid—of everybody's aid—to the underdeveloped world. Programs already under way, such as Paul Hoffman's "Special Fund" designed mainly to find out what the needs are (of which the United States is already pledged to contribute 40 per cent of the total), and the "Expanded Program of Technical Assistance," designed to supply specific help and knowledge, should be enlarged. The little-known U.N. program called "OPEX," which furnishes executive and administrative personnel to new countries until their own nationals can be trained, needs to be built up on a more extensive scale. The U.N. could greatly assist the new states in organizing their own requests for individual aid in the form of practicable programs that might be related to each other on a regional basis. Furthermore, international steps to steady the world commodity markets would be one of the most effective of long-term economic benefits to the raw-material producing countries.

Even if the international agencies for the supply of capital for plant and development expand their presently limited activities in tropical Africa, there will still be plenty of room for direct bilateral aid and for private capital investment from the United States and other countries. American help of this kind to subsaharan Africa has been puny. Aside from the special emergency funds made available for the Congo (totaling some thirty million dollars in 1960) American technical assistance for Africa south of the Sahara for the year ending June 30, 1960, amounted to but fifteen million dollars, an incredibly small figure in a four-billion-dollar foreign aid program. For the following year a "special program for tropical Africa" costing twenty million dollars was projected—characterized by the then Secretary of State Herter as "very modest." There is not too much time to readjust to a more realistic level of economic thinking both for the United Nations and ourselves; for the continent is moving so rapidly that the greater part of it will be free and the direction set before we realize what is happening. The quality and quantity of American representation in the new countries is also of vital importance. Fortunately, it has been improving in both respects. From twenty-one foreign service posts in the whole continent in 1950, the number has now grown (largely in subsaharan Africa) to forty and is still growing—incidentally, a much larger representation than the U.S.S.R.'s. The projected "youth corps" to serve as volunteers in Africa is a development of great promise. New programs for teacher training—one of the most acute of African needs—is another.

Since the war, the underdeveloped peoples in Asia and Africa and South America have been bursting the chains of their discontent. They see the material (if not spiritual) well-being of the other half of the world, and instead of following the time-honored practice of accepting their lot, they are demanding the good things of earth for themselves—and now. Yet, instead of narrowing, the gap is growing wider.

More than 800 million people have an average per capita income of less than one hundred dollars per year; and while this standard of living may be slowly rising, it is rising far less rapidly than that in the developed countries of the West. The rate of economic growth was ten dollars per person in the underdeveloped countries in the past ten years; the rate in the United States and Europe was twenty times that. An increasingly explosive problem is being created, worsened by a rapid rise in population and a failure to gear social, political and economic organization to meet these new conditions.

Whatever the size of our aid, it can only be successful if it is offered as assistance without strings, friendship without interference. The great advantage that we and the rest of the Free World have over Communist Russia and Communist China in offering such help is that we can give it without a political tie-in sale, while it is in the nature of their system that they cannot.

The true interest of America is that the people of Africa have the opportunity to make the great leap from neolithic to nuclear age in freedom, not into a new form of colonialism. Their interest and our interest are identical; it is one of the ironies and tragedies of history that we have allowed ourselves to become represented before the naïve peoples of the world as a citadel of reaction and an obstacle to change. Ours is in reality the most dynamic of all industrial societies; we, and not the Russians, are the revolutionists, with most to show—in economic welfare and in political freedom—for our economic and political revolutions. This is what we really have to offer, through the United Nations and through ourselves, to the underdeveloped and the uncommitted worlds.

To do so, we must maintain contact. That is the task ahead, in Africa (and Asia) and in the satellite world on Russia's European periphery as well. Just as it is to the most basic American interest that we help the new countries of Africa develop along their own lines, so it is essential to American interest to help Yugoslavia, Poland and the rest maintain as much independence in their special context as they can. The problems are different, and the solutions are different, but the prime requisite is the same: maintenance of contact.

One characteristically American way of accomplishing this has been through the work of private agencies. Just as American influence in the underdeveloped countries, particularly in Africa, has been in the past largely based on the extraordinary work of privately financed American educational missionaries, so American influence in Eastern Europe already owes much to the pioneering effort of private groups. In 1957 the Ford Foundation initiated a program of bringing to the United States and Western Europe professors, scholars and scientific and technical experts from Eastern Europe. A number of other private agencies and the United States government as well have joined in this work, which in its first three years was responsible for the visit of over three hundred foreigners (mostly Polish) for varying periods to university centers and scholarly institutes throughout the West. The Ford Foundation alone has to date allocated two million dollars to this program, which includes sending a small number of American scholars in economics, sociology and similar fields to Eastern Europe, and also distributing Western books and periodicals to Eastern European educational institutions.

Important as is this type of foreign exchange, it has to be supplemented by the enormously greater program of direct American aid to the satellite countries wherever possible. Here there is no question of operating through the United Nations, as in the case of Africa or Asia. Here we have to be on our own. Here it is rather a question of giving direct American assistance as an open and acknowledged move on the part of the United States government to strengthen and enlarge its ties with Poland and Yugoslavia, and to help them maintain as much independence of the U.S.S.R. as they can possibly achieve within the political realities.

We would be only deluding ourselves if we thought that such aid as we have in the past and will in the future render to these two major Communist countries will lessen their Communism. They are doing that, as we have seen, for themselves and in their own way. The hand of American friendship, expressed in dollars as well as in exchange programs, should be expected to exact a much more subtle influence—but an unmistakable influence nonetheless.

Its purpose is, or ought to be, a means of keeping open the channels of communication, to serve as a constant, unfailing reminder that the free democracies are interested in preserving intellectual, cultural, economic, commercial and political contact with any countries of Eastern Europe that will accept it. The rising threat of a truculent Communist China to the European Communist world, as well as to the non-Communist world, only makes the point more urgent.

There is an extraordinary reservoir of good will toward the United States among the peoples of such countries as Yugoslavia and Poland, that neither twenty years of Marxism, nor the speeches of obstructionist Congressmen whenever the aid question arises, nor the equally destructive speeches of Communist leaders have been able to obliterate. The lesser Communist states are suffused with a strong nationalist strain. They all are anxious to have their own window to the West and, depending on their physical location and their own inner strength, they are receptive to overtures from the West. They will not cease—at least in the foreseeable future—to be Communist. But their Communism can continue along that process of dilution that has long since been begun; and increasing contact with the Free World, the United States in particular, can hasten and intensify the process.

Whether in Eastern Europe or in subsaharan Africa, America needs the self-confidence to accept openly the friendship of countries of political outlook and economic structure totally different from ours. For nearly three centuries, our nation's most dominant characteristic in its greatest moments has been its dynamism, its vitality. In the more recent years of our "fat-dripping prosperity," as Sandburg called it, we have also been guilty of complacency, a luxury we can no longer afford. We are now in a world where American supremacy can no longer be taken for granted by ourselves, as it is no longer taken for granted by others. In this, the decade of decision, America faces its most decisive challenge and its most rewarding opportunity.

About the Author

John B. Oakes, of the Editorial Board of the *New York Times*, has all his life been a close observer of political developments throughout the world.

He recently spent nearly a year in Europe and Africa as recipient of a special award from the Carnegie Foundation. He is the first American winner of the Columbia-Catherwood prize for "responsible and enlightened international journalism."

After graduation from Princeton (magna cum laude and valedictorian) and Oxford (as a Rhodes Scholar), he began his newspaper career on the *Trenton Times* in 1936. The following year he went to Washington, where he covered Congress and the political campaigns for the *Washington Post*, and also wrote frequently on international affairs. His newspaper work was interrupted by five years of Army service. He received wartime decorations from the American, British and French governments.

Returning to journalism after the war, he joined the *New York Times* as editor of *The News of the Week in Review*. Since 1949, he has been on the *Times'* Editorial Board, and has also written extensively for the Sunday *Magazine* and the *Book Review*.

He lives in New York City with his wife and three daughters.

Date Due

MAR 5 '65			
MAY 28 '65			
FEB 28 '67			
DEC 5 1978			

The Edge of Freedom

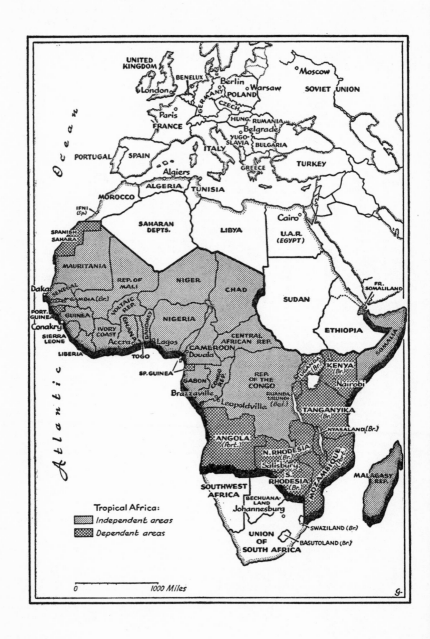

Tropical Africa:

Independent areas

Dependent areas

0   1000 Miles